What People Are Saying About
Miracle Relationships

To read a book on such a topic, a few things have to feel instinctively right for me. The criteria has to fit; I need to know that the author has walked the walk, the book has been recommended to me by someone whom I trust, and the book has landed on my lap or been intuitively guided in some way. I am delighted to say that all three boxes have been ticked with this little gem of a book, and therefore my heart can openly share and express with authenticity the deep wisdom and spirit that is enclosed within its pages.

Knowing John personally was of course a great start, as I have great respect for his own personal spiritual awakening and journey. He oozes presence, humility, humor and love. He most definitely walks his walk and demonstrates the joy and freedom that come from 'doing the work', so to speak. I have seen how his desire for a healthy, loving and holy relationship has unfolded for him and his wife, Anne. His commitment and dedication to honest, loving and clear communication has allowed for a deepening in all his relationships, and at the core is always his boundless fun, laughter and kindness. This is testament to his dedication for a joyful and beautiful life.

This book is a gift to those choosing to have healthy and authentic relationships. It helps the reader understand the purpose of any relationship and to trust that whatever has happened to date in their relationships there are immense possibilities to deepen into more fulfilling ones, forgive those that have turned sour, understand why they just didn't work out, or have been left heartbroken or bitter and are ready to heal. Let's face it, we've all been there in some form or another, and I know that personally the wisdom that is in this book would have saved me years of suffering and turmoil if I had known its principles earlier.

I highly recommend this book for anyone seeking the truth, who is ready to embrace another way of being in relationship. It can only benefit you and help you see more clearly, feel more deeply and let go of old limitations. Thank you, John, for walking the walk and sharing your heart, you are indeed a miracle and bright light for so many. With love and gratitude.
Ann-Marie Marchant, Multifaith minister, spiritual mentor, *A Course in Miracles* facilitator and author of *The Ripple of Awakening: A Mighty Companion on the Spiritual Awakening Journey*

This book is a great help in making relationships healthy and lasting. There are so many pearls of wisdom in John's book. "You can't have a deep, meaningful relationship with another until you have a deep, meaningful relationship with yourself." I find this so true. I had two marriages that fell apart, because I didn't have a loving relationship with myself. It took years of therapy, twelve-step recovery and *A Course in Miracles* to heal my mind, and be ready for a deep, loving relationship. I have one now, and I have been in heaven for twenty-two years. I wish this book had been available forty years ago. It would have saved me so much pain. It has taken me a lifetime to learn the lessons John presents in this beautiful book. If you apply the ideas to yourself and your relationships, it will change your life.
Dan Strodl, manager of Miracle Network and editor of *Miracle Worker* magazine

John Campbell's life itself is a Forgiveness Lesson à la *A Course in Miracles*. In other words, he has managed to wrap everyone and everything he has encountered in love, compassion and understanding, and in the warm glow of his profound acceptance everyone grows and heals. His book is a testament to that life, a beautifully wrought telling of a personal journey that becomes a collective allegory of emergence, wholeness and hope.

Maurice Taylor, MA Psychotherapy, Licensed Marriage and Family Therapist and co-author of *The New Couple: Why the Old Rules Don't Work and What Does*, published by HarperCollins

Everyone would benefit from reading this book before they enter an intimate relationship... I wish I had!!!

Gary Stevens, former England International, Brighton & Hove Albion FC, Tottenham Hotspur FC and Portsmouth FC professional footballer

Get this book if you want a quick read that will help you to reach a few 'aha' moments in terms of your personal relationships.

Dr. M. Samanta Laughton, author of *Punk Science*, published by John Hunt Publishing, and *The Genius Groove*, published by Paradigm Revolution Publishing

I am very fortunate, running an international organization, in that I meet many people who are committed to helping others change for the better. Of those people, some have a real skill for inspiring others to change. Of those few, some in turn have a gift to actually effect a great deal of change in the world. John Campbell is one of these rare people.

Tim Laurence, co-founder of Hoffman Institute UK and author of *You Can Change Your Life: A Future Different from Your Past with The Hoffman Process*, published by Hodder and Stoughton

John Campbell is one of those amazingly wise people. If you are fortunate enough to encounter him in your life you can consider yourself truly blessed.

Neil Crofts, author of *Authentic: How to Make a Living By Being Yourself* and *Authentic Business: How to Create and Run Your Perfect Business*, published by Capstone

This book is quite amazing in the way it enabled me to reflect on myself and the relationships in my life and make a difference! I actually had a few 'Eureka' moments when reading it, and it has helped me to understand myself and my relationship in a way I hadn't been able to do before. It's also such an easy read. I would recommend it to absolutely anyone for happier, healthier relationships in their life. Fascinating and unique! Thank you, John Campbell!

Caroline Adkin, Primary School Teacher

If you would like to heal any difficult relationships, or improve good ones, you will find a treasure chest of practical tools in this gem of a book. John Campbell synthesizes many years of his personal journey and studies to present clear, concise, practical tools for making your relationships the blessings they are intended to be. I especially value that John incorporates key principles from *A Course in Miracles* and other spiritual sources to take relationships to the highest level. Highly recommended for anyone seeking deeper peace, harmony, resolution, and joy in your most valued relationships. Many thanks for a golden gift!

Alan Cohen, author of the best-selling books *A Course in Miracles Made Easy, Are You as Happy as Your Dog?, The Dragon Doesn't Live Here Anymore* and *The Mystical Messiah*

Miracle Relationships

A Path to Freedom and Joy

Also By This Author

Innocent Sex: A Path from Guilt to Freedom
Dr. Anne & John Campbell
No ISBN as yet

Miracle Relationships

A Path to Freedom and Joy

John Campbell

BOOKS

Winchester, UK
Washington, USA

JOHN HUNT PUBLISHING

First published by O-Books, 2023
O-Books is an imprint of John Hunt Publishing Ltd., 3 East St., Alresford,
Hampshire SO24 9EE, UK
office@jhpbooks.com
www.johnhuntpublishing.com
www.o-books.com

For distributor details and how to order please visit the 'Ordering' section on our website.

ISBN: 978 1 80341 307 5
978 1 80341 308 2 (ebook)
Library of Congress Control Number: 2022912464

A CIP catalogue record for this book is available from the British Library.

Design: Lapiz Digital Services

UK: Printed and bound by CPI Group (UK) Ltd, Croydon, CR0 4YY
Printed in North America by CPI GPS partners

We operate a distinctive and ethical publishing philosophy in
all areas of our business, from our global network of authors to
production and worldwide distribution.

Contents

Dedication

I am dedicating this book to my wonderful partner in life, Dr. Anne Campbell. My co-teacher, my life partner, my great mate. For the wonderful courage and commitment she shows to her own growth and healing. For her indomitable spirit, constant laughter, fun and joy and for allowing me to be totally me. I love you.

Note from the Author

Please apply your inherent gift of discernment to the information given in this book, always remembering the wise words of Gautama Buddha.

Do not believe anything because it is said by an authority, or if it is said to come from angels, or from Gods, or from an inspired source. Believe it only if you have explored it in your own heart and mind and body and found it to be true.

Work out your own path, through diligence.

– Gautama Buddha

Foreword

Congratulations on discovering this little book!

As soon as I began reading the book you're holding in your hands, my immediate reaction was one of sheer excitement. I thought I had already learned a thing or two about relationships over the course of my life, but whilst reading the following pages I experienced true epiphanies. It seemed so obvious; I wondered how I hadn't realized it before.

There was a time when I would have quickly dismissed the principles in this book – I was not ready to see how and why circumstances in my life had unfolded as they had done. But thankfully, challenging circumstances prompted me to do further self-analysis, and provided the opportunity for me to experience the validity of the insights described in the following pages.

I will be forever grateful for the patience, honesty, and wisdom of the author. He has written something quite special here – a simple and compact, yet comprehensive guide that will be appreciated by all who are fortunate enough to read it. It is the kind of book you will read again over the years with increasing understanding and newly found meaning each time, as your own experiences broaden.

I have known the author for over forty years and have been privileged to witness the amazing changes he has made in his own life, the lives of his family and all those he comes into contact with, who are ready for a healthier way of relating to themselves and others. You see, the author is my father.

Understanding the principles in the pages that follow has undoubtedly enabled me to come through the most difficult times in my life; and has been beneficial not only to me but also to my children.

I trust that you will find this little book as valuable as I have.
Thank you, Dad, for everything.

Paul Campbell

Acknowledgements

Everyone comes into our life for a reason, some for a season and some for a lifetime and each person with whom I've ever come into contact has been both my teacher and my pupil. Often, when the lessons have been imparted, something might happen to cause the relationship to end and this is always perfectly 'arranged.' In other situations our relationship may be for a longer time, perhaps in a marriage, or long-term romantic relationship, which has come to a natural end. Similarly, if both parties have learned what they need to learn, sometimes it feels right to move on and such relationships come into the 'season' variety and can sometimes be quite difficult to bring to a conclusion.

Then there are the 'lifetime' relationships. These are generally parents, children and others with whom we often, and not always, find ourselves connected by bloodlines. These are the most powerful opportunities for growth as they are generally the ones with whom we have a deep emotional investment and which create numerous opportunities for forgiveness.

Kenneth Wapnick, a great teacher of *A Course in Miracles*, has written a book entitled *Parents and Children: Our Most Difficult Classroom* where he brilliantly describes the dynamics of these relationships.

I'd especially like to acknowledge all my 'lifetime' people for all they have taught me.

My parents, both now in Spirit. My mother, Joan Brotherton Campbell (née Spencer), and my surrogate father, Percy Robert Campbell. They both taught me the single most important lesson of my life – forgiveness – and gave me ample opportunity to practice this lesson, even though I didn't do so at the time.

Because I failed to forgive at the time I was a child – I then attracted 'love' relationships (what *A Course in Miracles* calls 'Special Relationships') in my adult life, which reflected back to me the various things I'd failed to forgive about my parents!

These lessons were reflected back to me by Sonia, Sherrill, Linnet, Mary, Anita, Kamala and, most recently, Annie. I'm grateful to them all for the growth opportunities they have all afforded me.

The other 'lifetime' people are, of course, my siblings. My half-sister Pam Price who was so supportive when we were children and my half-brother Peter Campbell, now in Spirit. I'm grateful to have had the opportunity to spend some close time with him before he passed away. I've been blessed with six fantastic children. Jacquie, Paul, Sarah, Lisa, David and Rachel have all been incredible teachers to me and I'm deeply grateful for them having chosen me to be their father… if that concept of children choosing their parents sounds a bit 'cuckoo' to you – please don't worry because it did to me when it was first suggested to me. However, my subsequent journey along the path has made it totally understandable!

It would feel incomplete here if I didn't mention my wonderful son-in-law, Ross Millard. He so clearly loves his wife, our daughter Sarah, and is an amazing father to their children, Halle and Rafe. What more could we ask? *A Course in Miracles* has a line in Chapter 6, "The Lessons of Love," which says, "Teach only love – for that is what you are," and I'm very grateful that Ross is in my life.

I've also been blessed with six (at the time of writing!) fantastic grandchildren. Mike, Sophia, Olivia, Halle, Josh and Rafe are all beautiful souls and also very wise teachers.

I've not experienced what it is like to have grandparents myself as I never met any of mine in my lifetime. I spoke a few brief words to my maternal grandfather, Geoffrey Spencer, over a crackly old-fashioned phone line to Canada when I was aged nine and that is the only contact I had with any of them. The others had all passed on before I was born.

So being a granddad has been something of a strange experience for me and I've often felt myself saying, "How do I 'do' being a grandparent?" But those master teachers, my grandchildren, have shown me a lot, and I'm so grateful for their teaching.

Finally my gratitude to all the friends, colleagues, teachers and clients who helped me in the creation of this book. So many who shared so openly with me about their own private relationship experiences made me realize how common these principles appear to be.

These include: Seana McGee and Maurice Taylor, Tim Laurence & Serena Gordon, Mary Chandler, Sue Lawson, Elaine Clark, Heather Pozzo, Penny Wilmot, Vicky Giles, Binnie Dansby, Patrick Houser, Frank & Caroline Runge, Roald & Brit Goethe, Gavin & Kelley Moran, the late Paul Carman, Mark Phillips, Jim Lindsay, Russ & Bridget Newlyn, Joyce & Gerry Gray, Gary Stevens, Kate Petrie, Ollie Clinch, Neil Cakebread and Anthony Benedict. To all my friends in the various ACIM groups I've been privileged to be a part of in many countries around the world, including our wonderful ACIM family. Dan Strodl, Teresa Yiannaco, Ian Patrick, Sharon Scarth, and all those who help at The Miracle Network and those who join their weekly Wednesday Meditation Group. Those wonderful Mighty Companions in the Study Group which Annie and I hold every Monday, including Noreen Kelty, Evie Armstrong, Kate McNeilly, Thui Prag, Elaine Clark, Jacquie Clavey-Weedon, Mahin Driskill, Melanie Bloch and, more recently, our son, Paul Campbell (who kindly also wrote the foreword to this book). Also to the inspirational teachers of the Course, whose books and workshops I have enjoyed so much: Carol Howe, Alan Cohen, David Hoffmeister and Gary Renard. Each of you has consistently reminded me, as I practice these principles, of the importance of humor and always remembering to laugh.

We have also enjoyed such wonderful connections from our lovely friends in Spain. Beatriz Canovas, Alberto Machin, Chiqui, Alehandro Amigote, Maria del Mar and Mario & Sabine in the tiny Canary Island of El Hierro; and Sue & Neal Dunkley, Karen Whitworth, Jenna Mincheva, Nerea Crespo and Montserrat Giner on the mainland of that beautiful country, Spain.

These acknowledgements would not be complete without a note of thanks to the team at John Hunt Publishing for having accepted my book and for their help in bringing it to fruition. Also to our dear friend and fellow *A Course in Miracles* teacher Ann-Marie Marchant, who introduced me to the John Hunt Publishing people. I am most grateful to all of you.

Finally, my deep gratitude goes to the late Doctors Helen Schucman and William Thetford. These were the original scribes of *A Course in Miracles*. Their dedication has helped change the minds of millions of people around the world, including myself, about the Truth of who we really are, and given us all the tools for creating inner peace. A peace which "Passeth all understanding" and is not dependent on anything in our outer lives. Their memory will live forever.

Introduction

My inspiration for finally putting this little book together was an experience I had in 2007. I was on a Greyhound bus trip from San Francisco, where I had been visiting a publisher, to Vancouver, Canada, to visit my partner at that time. The bus was full, and I ended up sitting next to a woman from Croatia. We started chatting, and the subject came around to what we both did for a living. I explained that I was a coach and both a teacher and student of a self-study course entitled *A Course in Miracles*, and that, because it so greatly helped me understand my life and my relationships, I was passionate about sharing this information with others. This prompted the woman to describe her own, seemingly dismal, relationship history. She was interested to know if I could shed any light as to the reasons for all the heartache she had encountered. We didn't have long to go to our destination, and so I described, as briefly as I was able, the purpose of relationships, the standard route that most of these take, and the reasons behind this route. With the back of the headrest of the person in front acting as a mini blackboard, I used my index figure to describe what a healthy family system looks like (see the first diagram in chapter 8).

After my very brief, impromptu 'seminar,' this woman looked at me in astonishment and declared, "You have just explained my whole life in twenty minutes, knowing barely anything about me! You should write a book!" I thanked her, and we each went our separate ways. It was a turning point for me, however, because the seed that had been sown in my mind finally took root. Prior to that experience, I had similar encounters with many other people of various nationalities and ages who prompted me in one way or another to put together what you now have in your hands.

My intention is to provide a simple, short introductory guide to open a window of awareness about the nature of intimate relationships, and how you can make these unions lasting, healthy and fulfilling in your life. At the end of the book, you will find a comprehensive resource section to assist you in furthering your learning if you so desire.

There are literally thousands of books available on this subject which espouse similar theories to those contained in these pages. Many of these are excellent resources, and some are bulky and can be overwhelming – especially for youngsters and those who have had no exposure to family system theories or other psychological concepts. I also trust that this book will satisfy those who – like me – tend to 'want it and want it now.'

Though I have had excellent training and worked with some of the finest family therapists available, my greatest contribution to this subject is my very own, sometimes excruciatingly painful, experience – both as a child growing up in an unhealthy family system and also as a spouse and parent in similar systems. In the world of relationships, I could say, "I've seen it, done it, and have the T-shirt," many times over! Knowing well that I can only assist others to the extent that I have healed myself, I am also committed to continually working on and furthering my own healing.

As you read this book, I encourage you to keep an open mind, see what makes sense to you, take what helps you, and leave the rest – although I recommend that you avoid dismissing anything out of hand. I often find myself saying of some teaching I may have heard long ago, "Oh, now I see what they meant. Now it makes perfect sense," when before I may have considered the teaching complete rubbish.

The fact that you now have this little book in your hands is evidence that you have some important use for it. There can only be one other possible reason for you to have picked it up, and it may be because you have a close friend or someone you know who has need of the information it contains. If this is the case, then you will know intuitively, and you will also know what to do with it.

If there is one lesson that is continually being proven to me every day of my life it is this: nothing, absolutely nothing in this world of ours happens by accident. You may find that your mind struggles to understand the concepts discussed in these pages. You may even have difficulty reading the book. If there is any impediment of any type, I recommend that you do not force yourself. Put it among your other books and I guarantee that a time will come when this one will mysteriously pop into your mind, or even fall onto the floor in front of you one day. That will be the sign that you are ready to receive the information it contains. There is a wonderful wise saying, "When the student is ready – the teacher appears," and this too has been proven over and over again.

Early in my journey of awakening, I experienced this concept first hand when a good friend recommended I read a book called *The Celestine Prophecy* by James Redfield. I am a very eager and passionate learner so I immediately purchased the book – and the audio version too, just for good measure! As soon as they arrived I excitedly inserted the audio cassette into my car's sound system and started listening to the first chapter. I remember thinking, "What is this rubbish?" Notice how judgmental I was? It may even be the type of response that sounds familiar to you. Well anyway, not being easily deterred, when I arrived home I started reading the paperback version, thinking I may understand the written word more easily. No such luck. It all still seemed like gibberish. In disgust at what I thought was a waste of my money, I carelessly threw the book into a bedroom cupboard. Meanwhile, I continued my learning and one day, about six months later, I found myself looking for something in that same cupboard. As I rummaged through the contents, the copy of *The Celestine Prophecy* fell at my feet.

I could almost hear it calling to me, "You're ready now. Please pick me up and read me!" I followed the sign and listened to my burgeoning inner voice. I picked the book up and settled down to try again.

The same book that only six short months earlier I had condemned as "rubbish" was now being devoured at the rate of knots. This time I could not put it down! My wife and children had gone to visit family and were out for the whole day. By the time they returned I had read the book from cover to cover and ordered the next book in James Redfield's series of *The Ten Insights*. When I'd first attempted to read the book I simply did not yet have the 'building blocks' in place to understand it. The student was not yet ready – so the teacher could not appear!

I particularly wanted this book to be small enough to fit in your purse or pocket when you're out on that all important first date. That's when people are generally on their best behavior, so if even the faintest of alarm bells start ringing in your head, but your little inner critic whispers, "Oh don't be silly, that's just your imagination! And besides, you're too sensitive and your standards are way too high," you can make a hasty dash for the restroom, armed with this little book. If a quick glance at the words on these pages confirms that your date is not a suitable match for you, politely – and without hesitation – make your exit. And then, when you get back to the safety of your home, you can congratulate yourself for 'seeing the hole in the road and walking around it instead of falling into it.'

The following verse, which I was given during my counselling training, succinctly describes many of our relationship experiences:

I once walked down the road and fell into a hole I hadn't seen.

I was very confused. It took a long, long time to climb out.

I walked down the road and fell into the same hole. I just hadn't seen it. I was very confused but eventually climbed out.

I walked down the road and saw the hole and still fell into it. I couldn't believe it. This time I quickly climbed out.

I walked down the road and saw the hole and walked around it.

I took another road.

Chapter 1

The Real Purpose of Intimate Relationships

Many of us have been subtly brainwashed by our multi-generational patterning, the media, and various other means to believe that the goal of relationships is to find our 'one and only,' fall madly in love, get married, settle down, have a family, and live happily ever after. Movies are made, songs are sung, and poetry and books are written eulogizing this magical thing called 'romance' and 'love,' underscoring how when we find the 'right one,' we will feel complete and secure.

The reality is very different. I eventually learned that I couldn't possibly have a deep, meaningful relationship with another until I had developed a deep, meaningful, relationship with myself. Until I found out who I really was, discovered what made me tick, and developed a deep sincere love for me, I couldn't possibly relate in a healthy way and truly love another.

Most of my relationship history was spent trying to get love from somewhere outside of myself, and it always ended in heartache and disappointment.

As a child, I desperately sought the love of my alcoholic mother, but it was impossible for her to love me when alcohol was the primary relationship in her life and she was riddled with self-loathing.

This set up a pattern in me at an early age, whereby I continually sought love from women who were, for one reason or another, 'unavailable.' And, of course, I was similarly 'unavailable' to them. I continued this pattern of searching for love outside of myself into my late fifties, until I came upon the information I am now sharing with you.

Very simply, the real purpose of intimate relationships is to jointly, in partnership with each other, assist in healing the apparent wounds of childhood and develop a deepening sense of self-love and self-forgiveness, which in turn will facilitate a sense of healthy interdependency. The means for this process will be explored later in this book.

Chapter 2

The Essential Ingredients for Successful Relationships

There are two ingredients that, in my experience, are absolutely essential if a relationship is to stand a chance of surviving while a couple negotiate all the vicissitudes of daily family and working life. These two ingredients are better referred to as 'chemistries,' for they can never be consciously manufactured or learned or developed in a relationship the way other attributes like patience, tolerance, and consideration can be.

These two chemistries are:
- Physical or Sexual Chemistry
- Best Friend Chemistry

I encourage you to read two books, *The New Couple* and *What's the State of Your Union?*, by two wonderful relationship counsellors and masters in their field, Seana McGee and Maurice Taylor.

They have brilliantly described in great detail the meaning of these two essential ingredients. I will touch on a couple of relevant points here.

Sexual chemistry is different from lust and can frequently be confused with it. I'm defining lust as the existence of a strong sexual energy that enables you to have sex with someone without necessarily finding them particularly physically attractive.

This sometimes occurs when individuals are under the influence of alcohol or drugs. When I refer to sexual chemistry, I am referring to a situation where two people have a strong sexual attraction and each finds the other physically beautiful.

When someone is under the influence of any recreational drug, such as alcohol or marijuana, or even prescription mood-altering drugs, such as antidepressants or tranquilizers, a sense of physical and emotional euphoria can be mistaken for sexual and best friend chemistry in a relationship.

The balance of your mind is disturbed, and so it's no wonder many unhealthy decisions, not purely relationship choices, are made in those states.

Here is an example of just such a decision I made: Once, after a boozy lunch, I went out and paid cash for a brand-new Jaguar XJS two-seater sports car. Now you may ask, "What's wrong with that if you can afford it?" Well you're right, except that in my case I was married with four little children – not to mention I'm six feet five inches tall and struggled to even sit in the driver's seat. If I had been completely sober, and therefore the balance of my mind had not been disturbed, I would never have done it. When I was sober the following day I sheepishly returned it to the showroom at a large financial loss!

So both sexual chemistry and best friend chemistry need to be present at the beginning of the relationship. Despite the fact that they can, and frequently do, wane over the course of a long-term relationship, if they are not both present at the beginning, the relationship will invariably flounder at some stage or other.

No amount of therapy can create the missing chemistries, but quality therapy will certainly aid in reigniting the chemistries if they were originally present but have begun to wane. If the chemistries were never there to begin with or the partners are simply not compatible, quality therapy then becomes invaluable in any dissolution of the relationship.

You may be surprised to learn that numerous couples embark on a serious and committed relationship without one or the other of these chemistries present. In some cases, neither of them is present. I will refer to such unions from now on as 'mismatched,' as that is really what they are from the outset and therefore stand little hope of mutual fulfillment.

You may be asking, "Why would anyone couple up with someone with whom they did not have both these chemistries?" It's more common than you may realize, and the most likely reason is that they're recreating what they witnessed in their parents' relationship. We invariably repeat these unfulfilling scenarios simply because they feel familiar to us. Note that the word familiar stems from the word family.

Mismatched unions also occur commonly in cultures where arranged marriages are the norm. In these unions, parents and/or grandparents choose the mates for their children. It is important to mention here that this does not mean that every arranged marriage is a mismatch. If the young couple is really fortunate and they have those two chemistries present when they partner up, they can be grateful for their parents' choice.

Sadly, however, many such unions are based on the man's suitability to provide financial support and the woman's ability to provide children.

Those may well be important ingredients, but without the two essential chemistries being present, the couple is unlikely to be able to create a mutually fulfilling relationship regardless of the longevity of the union.

Very often, in mismatched unions such as these, the parent-child relationship takes precedence over the couple's relationship with each other and becomes the primary relationship in the family. The resulting dysfunction may have long-lasting consequences that have been described in some circles as 'emotional incest.' This may sound like a pretty harsh description, but I think it needs to be harsh because of the deep damage this syndrome inflicts on everyone involved.

Even though arranged marriages are not nearly as common as in previous generations, the children of these unions have had the mismatch union modelled to them. These children then grow up and may still unconsciously be attracted to a similar mismatch partner, despite the fact that theirs was a choice seemingly of their own and not of their parents.

If they go on to have children, the same pattern may be continued, and so the painful tentacles of these mismatched unions insidiously work their way down through generation after generation until someone breaks the chain.

Interestingly, when a mismatched couple has more than one child, very often one of the children grows up and chooses a mismatch partner, while the others choose partners with whom both chemistries are present. It's almost as though, until the mismatch of the parents is openly explored and acknowledged and brought to the conscious awareness of all concerned, one of the offspring from that union needs to keep the memory of the mismatch in that family system.

It is important to remember that none of this is happening consciously. Another situation that sometimes results in a mismatch is when a woman gets pregnant, and then the couple decides they should get married or couple up for the sake of the unborn child. If both chemistries were not present at the start of the relationship, the two main ingredients for a mutually fulfilling relationship experience will still be missing.

The absence of one or both chemistries at the start of any relationship will likely manifest in a breakdown of the relationship somewhere further down the road.

Once again, when the children from such a union grow up, they may repeat that pattern of choosing an incompatible mate, and so the chain continues. This is why I strongly encourage you to closely examine your parents' relationship. It will give you important insight into any familial patterns, providing you with the opportunity to work through and break any such pattern that doesn't lead to a mutually fulfilling relationship.

I have spoken to hundreds of individuals who have described their parents' relationship as a mismatch, and the most common thread among the descriptions was the existence of extreme rage in both of the partners.

This often stems from the mistaken belief that they are stuck and are helpless victims in the situation. They have told themselves that they have to stay, often for the 'sake of the children.'

In some cases, this rage is very overt in one or both of the parents; that is to say, one or both of them 'acted out' the rage. This is often termed 'aggressive anger,' and it is characterized by shouting, screaming, hitting, poking, aggressive pointing, interrogating, threatening, ridiculing, and condemning.

There are also cases where one or both of the partners 'acted in' this rage. This is sometimes referred to as 'passive/aggressive anger.' It may look very different, but it is no less devastating to all involved. It frequently results in depression (anger and other emotions are being de-pressed) and is often characterized by alcohol and/or drug dependency.

Instead of facing the painful truth of their mismatch, the individuals concerned will often numb the pain of the unfulfilling and lonely relationship with excessive alcohol use, illegal drugs, legal drugs like antidepressants, or excessive working. This passive/aggressive anger is often characterized by sarcasm, ridicule, criticism, put-downs, teasing, unfavorable comparing with others, accusing, blaming, silent treatment, and withholding.

An apparent 'happiness' may even seem to be present with excessive laughter and almost habitual 'joking.' When you look more closely, however, the laughter is often not natural and easy flowing with a joyous energy but is subtly tinged with ridicule and judgment.

Many people ask, "How can we know when we have sexual and best friend chemistries?" It's a very good question,

19

especially since lust is so often confused with sexual chemistry. I would like to share a true story, one I now think of as the very first advice I received on this subject of distinguishing between sexual chemistry and lust.

I was a seventeen-year-old, naïve Navigating Cadet in the Merchant Navy. I was still a virgin and with no romantic relationship experience whatsoever from which to draw. I was talking about various life matters with my Senior Second Officer of the Watch as we peered out from the bridge into the black of the night, steaming along in the balmy waters of the Persian Gulf.

Second Officer John Wilkins was clearly a man of the world. He was Intelligent, seemingly self-confident and with a keen sense of humor. He also had that old Etonian, upper-class English accent that alludes to superior knowledge. He seemed to be the perfect person to advise me on this question that was bugging my young mind.

"Sir," I started nervously, "how do you know when you're really in love?" I was eager to hear his response because I had never witnessed my parents being 'in love' with each other, as I had imagined the term to mean.

He turned away from the warm breeze and looked me straight in the eyes. "Campbell," he started with great authority, "When you can witness your partner sitting on the loo and you still feel a sense of warmth and tenderness to her with no sense of disgust or revulsion – and she feels the same about you in the reverse situation – then you know you are both in love!" Fifty years later, I still believe he hit upon a great description of what I have come to understand as 'sexual chemistry.' It is as though your two bodies love each other so much, almost independently of your minds, and absolutely nothing about your bodies has the ability to make you reject them. It does not matter what size or shape they may turn into. It does not matter what situation you see your mate in, it is impossible to feel any aversion or disgust at it or any of its functions. This is what I have come to experience as sexual chemistry. I can tell you that in my relationship history, I surely knew when this was not present and lust had taken over!

A Compatibility Theory (Dancing to the Same Tune)

I have a simple theory about 'compatibility' based on the understanding that we are all energetic beings. We are vibrational beings; our bodies and minds, like everything else in the universe, are constantly vibrating at various frequencies. When someone says, "I get good vibes from that person," what it really means is that those two people, at some level of their being, are vibrating at the same, or at least a similar, frequency to each other.

In David Hawkins' excellent book, *Power vs. Force*, he details how he was able to calibrate various emotions using kinesiology. His work led me to develop my own theory on how this information affects human relationships.

My theory is that in our connections with each other, we have the opportunity to interact at five different levels: the physical, the mental, the emotional, the spiritual, and finally the soul level. I can imagine that an absolute perfect match is when two people are vibrating at the same or very similar frequencies at all five levels of being.

Imagine how deeply satisfying such a union would be. I suggest that this is quite rare, and when couples do experience such a situation, they may refer to each other as their 'twin flame.'

The challenge in intimate relationships is that, as with all vibrating elements, frequencies can change. As Dr. Hawkins explains, different emotions have different vibrations. Anger, resentment, hatred, jealousy, apathy, and sadness are all lower vibrational frequencies; whereas joy, happiness, gratitude, compassion, and forgiveness are of higher frequencies.

21

When one partner makes a decision to start doing some kind of therapy or personal development work, and the other partner does not, it can create a disturbance within the relationship. The frequency of the partner doing the inner clearing starts to change, and so the couple no longer vibrates at the same frequency.

What is put into the body in the way of food and drink also affects a person's vibration. Alcohol, tobacco, and drugs (including prescription medicines) have a lower vibration than water, natural fruit juices, and fresh vegetables. I am not judging any of these things as good or bad – it's only that they vibrate at different frequencies.

I find it interesting to note that in marriages involving a partner who is an alcoholic or drug addict, very few of these marriages survive when the addict gets sober or off the drugs if the other partner does not decide to do some kind of clearing work of their own.

In my opinion, the reason for that statistic is usually because the sober partner's vibration changes so dramatically that the other partner gets angry. This difference in vibration means they no longer resonate with each other. They are no longer 'dancing to the same tune' so to speak.

Let us now examine the predictable stages that relationships take. Interestingly, my experience of these stages is not restricted to intimate relationships; a similar pattern seems to unfold in all relationships, including friends and work colleagues.

Chapter 3

The Three Stages of Relationships

There are three stages most relationships will follow:

Stage 1: Euphoric/Honeymoon/Intoxication
What *A Course in Miracles* refers to as "a special relationship."

Stage 2: Power Struggle or Conflict
What *A Course in Miracles* refers to as the beginning of the acceptance that "there must be a better way." ACIM T-2.III

Stage 3: Peaceful or Interdependent Stage
When the relationship is accepted as a learning device. When the relationship partners ask for help and begin understanding each other and begin taking 100% responsibility for each other's actions. *A Course in Miracles* refers to this as a Holy Relationship.

The **first stage** is that well-known feeling of bliss and euphoria. Neither can do any wrong, or if they do, it is quickly overlooked. This stage has a finite shelf life. It has to end; as much as we hate the thought, the 'drug' must wear off. The length of this stage can be as short as a month or as long as a couple of years, but rarely will exceed this. Whatever the individual time experience is, as night follows day, the couple will then enter the second stage.

The **second stage** is characterized by competition, power struggles, and varying degrees of conflict. It is important to note here that this second stage only seems to develop after there is some kind of commitment to the relationship. This could be in the form of an official marriage, or the couple beginning to cohabit, or if the woman gets pregnant and a decision is made to keep the child. It's almost as though an invisible force is saying, "Okay, now that there's a commitment, we can start letting the crappy stuff come out!" It is during this stage when one of three scenarios usually occurs.

The conflict may be so severe that the couple discontinue the relationship and go their separate ways.

One of the partners may put up the white flag of surrender and become the victim, while the other becomes the persecutor or controller. In this situation, there is often a 'My way or the highway' attitude from the controller and a feeling of compliance and victimization from the other party. Make no mistake though – both find this scenario miserable.

You may have seen cases where a couple has stayed together for even fifty years, but the two are so clearly miserable with each other, it's written all over their faces, and often one or both will turn to alcohol to blot out the pain and loneliness.

In some cases, partners can even unconsciously develop an illness and die in order to 'leave' the unhappy union. My own experiences have continually shown me that whenever my actions are not in alignment with what my heart is feeling, and I fail to take remedial action and do what my heart is begging for, eventually 'life' takes the action required. It is often far more painful in the long run.

John Lennon so astutely captured people's camouflaged pain in the words of his song *Crippled Inside*. Sadly, couples who imagine they are stuck in an unhappy relationship often have no idea how to remedy their situation. We will explore what else makes them endure such misery later.

The couple is aware that they have the necessary chemistry to go the long haul, and they make a joint decision to get some help. 'Help' may be in the form of therapy, reading books like this one, or going to workshops, but they have made the commitment to do whatever it takes to heal their 'stuff' and make a go of their relationship.

When the third scenario above happens, and the couple clearly started with the two necessary chemistries, they stand a good chance of enjoying the **third and final stage** of peace and healthy interdependence. They are now each whole individuals experiencing healthy interdependency rather than unhealthy codependency. They are no longer relying on each other to fill an apparent void in the other. And on the occasions when they may slip back into that destructive mode of thinking and behaving, they have the awareness of what is happening and have tools to deal with it. This is what *A Course in Miracles* refers to as a Holy Relationship.

Now they are both taking 100% responsibility for all their feelings and experiences. They are both following their life's purpose, mutually supported by the other, and the bond between them is ever strengthening. The feeling of neediness and insecurity previously present in the relationship has now become the exception rather than the former rule. They are both more consistently aware that the other partner is never responsible for any of their feelings, and they understand when their mate is simply triggering an unhealed memory from the past, deeply buried in their unconscious mind.

How often have you taken the 'exit' route at stage one, only to find that your next relationship, after the initial euphoric stage, inexplicably begins to look very similar to your previous experience – even though the person is different? Eventually, most people wake up to this and then start to ask themselves, "Why does this happen to me every time?" We will now examine the answer to that question.

Chapter 4

Why Does This Keep Happening to Me?

Our whole life is a university of learning and we are constantly being 'inner guided' to become what we really want to become. Our ultimate goal, in my opinion, is to reach a point where we no longer search for love, compassion, and forgiveness outside of ourselves – because we have learned to source it from within.

The way this university works is that it will keep presenting you situations and people that trigger you, in varying degrees, into feeling all the feelings you have suppressed in your past. Holding on to old hatreds can cause many problems for us – including physical illness – because what the mind represses, the body expresses. I have found that, until I reach a point of total forgiveness of my past and the people in it, the University of Life will keep sending people into my life who will remind me of the original ones I'm still resenting.

Intimate relationships are the greatest tool for uncovering these. So the problems we experience in our life are really only lessons we haven't learned properly yet. We will usually recreate in our adult relationships a replay of our childhood until we decide to delve in and do this essential forgiveness work. Often these replayed relationships show up not only in our intimate partner relationships but also in our working and day-to-day interaction with the world in general.

My path of real forgiveness did not begin until I was fifty-four years of age and I undertook an amazing piece of work called The Hoffman Process. (See more about this work in a later chapter.) On the first day, my Australian teacher, Craig, wrote on the flip chart: "Wherever I go – Whoever I see – I see Mummy and Daddy, and they see me." This blew my mind at first, but later I came to accept that nearly all the conflict in my adult life was with people who were exhibiting similar patterns of behavior that had annoyed me about my parents.

That is what I meant earlier when I explained that the purpose of relationships is to heal our childhood wounds and to practice forgiveness. And remember the last part of Craig's statement – "and they see me". It is so important to realize that the partner to whom you are attracted also has the opportunity to forgive their own childhood experiences – and is attracted to you for the same reasons. So, in fact, you are perfectly matched for healing to take place.

The trick though is to do the bulk of your deep healing work before you get into a serious committed relationship so that you have cleared the really heavy baggage of your past and will not need your partner to give you that heavy stuff in your love relationship. You will always have 'stuff' that keeps popping up to clear, but the really heavy stuff can be cleared with whatever type of healing works best for you.

To give you an example of what I mean in the above paragraph, let us imagine that you were physically beaten and severely abused by one or both of your parents or caregivers. If you do not get professional help to work through all that abuse baggage and come to a sense of peace around the perpetrators before committing in a relationship, you will either unconsciously attract someone who will abuse you in a similar way, or – and this can be the tough thing to accept – you will become the abuser, and that abuse can be subtle and difficult to spot for an untrained eye.

One thing I know is true: you either 'work it out,' or you'll 'act it out,' and the consequences for all concerned, especially helpless children, can be devastating and are likely to be passed on.

As explained earlier, the problem is that these childhood wounds don't come to the surface at the beginning of the relationship!

When all the endorphins are flowing and you are both still in the intoxication or honeymoon stage, they are numbed out. And then, when you are nicely committed and truly hooked – usually within the first two years – bang! Suddenly these two little kids come out screaming, "Now you can be the mummy or daddy I always wanted and never had!" Then the battles commence and the sparks fly. If nothing is done in the way of getting some therapeutic help, one or the other of the couple puts up the white surrender flag and takes on the victim role while the other fulfills the role of persecutor. Both, however, are exceedingly unhappy in these roles; it's always a two-way street.

Alternatively, one partner may decide enough is enough and leave, vowing never to make the same mistake again. However, without quality inner work, they will eventually get into a new relationship, only for the same sequence of events to replay. Or, they may declare, "That's it, I have no desire to have a partner. I'm very happy on my own, doing my own thing."

I'm sorry to disillusion those who may have taken that stance, but my experience is that part of being human is to innately desire a committed, intimate relationship with a significant other person.

In this case, the reality often is that the person is terrified at the thought of the same thing happening again and would rather not take the risk.

Once you have become conscious of this process and made a commitment to heal your wounds, you will be amazed how life will, seemingly accidentally, present situations that will trigger every major trauma – and minor ones later, too – which you experienced while growing up. The purpose is to give you the opportunity to feel all the emotions you suppressed at the time, as it may not have been safe for you to do so at that young age.

It will usually be your beloved partner who will facilitate these triggers. The good news is that once you learn to recognize when you're being triggered, you can tap into the real source of your feelings instead of having the knee-jerk reaction of blaming your partner for your feelings. In fact, you may even end up thanking your partner for bringing these past traumas to your conscious mind and presenting you with the opportunity to heal.

Chapter 5

How to Know When You're Being Triggered by an Incident from Your Past

The easiest way to spot when you're being triggered by an unconscious memory from the past is when your reaction to an event, person, or incident is way out of proportion to the present-moment situation. The reaction will often resemble that of a child, and that's because it's coming from the unhealed 'child' part of the person.

Here's an exaggerated example: if your partner accidentally steps on your toe in the shopping mall, and you start screaming and shouting at them and slap them in the face, I would suggest that you could consider that reaction as being out of proportion to the event. I know that this is an exaggerated example, but hopefully it gives you an idea of what I mean. Now I will describe some real-life examples of these triggers or flashbacks.

Real-Life Example 1

One evening, Bob and Sandra were entertaining guests for dinner. Bob was sitting talking to the guests, and Sandra was at the cooker checking on the meal. The telephone near her rang, so she picked it up and answered the call. Later, Bob inquired as to who had called, and Sandra explained that a friend had called to invite them for dinner the following week.

This friend had originally been introduced to them by Bob through his circle of contacts, and when his wife explained who had called, he immediately felt enraged and aggressively questioned his wife as to why she had not called him to the phone since this person was 'his' friend! (Note the 'childlike' element of his reaction – the quick clue that it is not about the present.) Bob was quite agitated and angry, but thankfully both he and Sandra had done a lot of joint healing work and were both aware of these processes. His wife pointed out to him that he might be experiencing a painful incident from his childhood. That immediately helped Bob to focus again on present time, and he quickly realized that he had been triggered by a past memory.

He took a minute on his own to reflect and uncover the original incident – the real source of his anger. Within moments, the original scene surfaced in Bob's conscious mind. When he was a young boy, between the ages of twelve and fifteen, his friends used to phone his home to invite him to go to the park and play football with them. Bob's mother, who was very controlling, always answered the phone first and lied to his friends, telling them that he was not at home.

That was because she had claimed Bob as her 'companion' – a very unhealthy setup – as his father had left her, and she didn't want Bob going out and 'leaving' her on her own.

When Bob went to school the following day, his pals told him that they had had a great game of football in the park and were sorry that he was out when they called. Of course Bob felt furious that he had missed this healthy fun with his friends as a result of his mother's lies.

He was unable to express all these feelings at the time for fear of upsetting his mum, and so the incident, together with his feelings of anger and resentment towards his mother, were buried deep in the annals of his subconscious mind. When the situation on the night of their dinner party triggered that memory and the buried feelings associated with it, Sandra received all the anger which was really meant for his mother forty years before!

Real-Life Example 2

Geoff was shopping with his new bride, Monica, in a mall when she realized that she had forgotten to pay for some cosmetics she had purchased at the counter a few moments previously.

Monica was the most honest, kind, and generous person you could wish to meet, the sort of person who would give you her last cent and would no more think of stealing anything than fly to the moon.

Before she had realized this mistake, she and Geoff had been blissfully holding hands. However, as soon as she explained what she had inadvertently done, Geoff completely shut down. He didn't want anything to do with her, wanted to get as far away as possible from her, and certainly no longer wanted to hold her hand! Again, notice the 'childlike' behavior.

Geoff was immediately aware that he was experiencing a trigger from the past and explained to his wife that he needed to go off for a minute to uncover the original incident and clear it. He moved to a quiet part of the store, sat down on a chair, and went back to his childhood memories. Within a few minutes, the original scene came flooding back to Geoff's conscious mind.

When he was only eight years old, his mother, quite a disturbed woman, used to take him on shoplifting expeditions. Geoff explained that he used to have to fill a bag with goods from the shelves while his mother kept the shopkeeper distracted looking for other things. Imagine the terror, anger, and helplessness he would have felt at that age. Unable to express all those emotions, like Bob in the previous example, Geoff buried them deep in his unconscious mind only for them to surface all those years later in a Texas mall. As soon as he had completed the exercise, all the love and closeness with his wife returned. He was able to share with her what his feelings were really about and explain that it had absolutely nothing to do with her.

Real-Life Example 3

Kathy was into complementary medicine and was training to be an acupuncturist. Her husband, Richard, was not really into complementary medicine but was more than happy to support his wife's interest. One day, however, he suddenly got very angry with his wife when she suggested that they rent a motorbike on holiday (vacation) to tour around. Richard raised his voice and even became tearful, accusing Kathy of being irresponsible and voicing his concern that if they were to have an accident and he became seriously injured, his wife would start practicing acupuncture on him instead of getting him to the nearest hospital for medical help.

Kathy knew immediately that this childlike reaction was the result of an old trauma locked in her husband's unconscious mind. She gently asked her husband what had happened when he was young to trigger this behavior. When Richard thought about her question, an old memory surfaced of when his father had an accident with Richard on the back of his motorcycle when he was only three. Richard's leg was caught in the wheel and badly cut. He was in terrible pain and there was a lot of blood, but instead of going immediately to a hospital, Richard's dad just wrapped a piece of cloth around his leg and went on to do his fishing at a pond! Once Richard was able to recall this painful memory, he lost the aggression towards his wife. He knew that she would never attempt to mend a smashed-up body with acupuncture, and he let go of the irrational fear of renting a motorbike to tour on their holiday.

Real-Life Example 4

Jennifer and Mike were a very friendly and outgoing couple who got on well with everyone in the neighborhood. They had lived in the same house since their marriage and had no problems with their neighbors. One day, the neighbor to the left of their house came around and complained that Jennifer's music was too loud and politely requested her to reduce the volume. Jennifer became very angry and vowed not to speak to this man again. She also insisted that her husband join her in this campaign of silence. Once again see the 'childlike' response to the situation. They eventually sold their home and moved to another area.

Soon after moving into their new property Jennifer, once again, fell out with the neighbor to the left of their house over a request to put up a fence. Despite her husband, Mike, being quite relaxed about the situation, Jennifer became obsessive and insisted that Mike and their little boy have no contact with this neighbor and their child. This reaction was, again, similar to that of a young child and a clear example that an old painful experience was being triggered in Jennifer.

The memory was a very painful one. When she was around nine years of age, Jennifer's mum had an affair with their next door neighbor and this was discovered by Jennifer's dad.

Her father became extremely bitter and berated Jennifer if she as much spoke to the neighbor or their children. Imagine the anger, hurt and sadness Jennifer would have experienced at that time – especially as her mum eventually left the family home to make a new life with this man.

Those deep memories were stored in her unconscious mind and therefore in her adult life she unconsciously attracted conflict from neighbors – on exactly the same side of her house as the neighbor who had the affair with her mum. When Jennifer realized how she was being triggered – she also realized that her older sister had frequently fallen out with neighbors during her married life.

I hope that these examples of flashbacks – or what psychologists sometimes call 'transference' – have given you a basic understanding of how these moments of overreaction, when we do not have this knowledge and understanding, can cause havoc in our interpersonal relationships.

One of the lessons in *A Course in Miracles*, Lesson No: 5, is that "I am never upset for the reason I think" and these examples explain what that lesson means.

Often, simply by bringing the original incident to the conscious mind, that process can heal the memory and return us to a sense of present moment peace. Sometimes, however, deeper work may be required whereby we have an opportunity to express all our emotions to a benevolent witness – a safe friend or therapist – who bears witness to the feelings we were unable to express at the time of the original incident.

People often ask, "When do I know I have healed this?" The answer is simple: when you can recall the original incident in your mind and no longer experience any 'charge' or emotional reaction to the memory. It's that simple. And don't concern yourself too much with this question because, rest assured, life will bring about further similar incidents until it is fully released and forgiven.

I should also explain here that this thing called 'transference' is not gender specific. What that means is that a male can sometimes trigger an aspect of the mother, and similarly a woman can sometimes trigger an aspect of the father. This can often be quite confusing.

A woman pondering the negative behavior of her male partner might find herself thinking, "But my father was never like that – in fact, he was quite the opposite," when in fact it was her mother's behavior her husband was repeating. The same applies to a man thinking his wife's behavior is nothing like his mum's – when it is his father's behavior the wife is repeating.

My experience is that it is the behavior of the parent or principal caregiver who we perceived (and do remember that it is always only our perception) as being the most negatively impactful that we will see repeated by others in our life. Of course, most of us experienced negativity from both of our parents, but the tendency is to minimize or even deny any negativity from one or the other of them; we do this as kids because we need to make up a 'fantasy' story to help us to feel safe.

Chapter 6

9 Steps to Help You Avoid Repeating Relationship Mistakes

'The secret is in the selection' is a lovely phrase I like to remind people to think about when embarking on a search for a partner. Isn't it amazing that before we purchase a house or a car, we take the greatest of care by employing the services of professionals to investigate many different aspects of our intended purchase. But when it comes to arguably the single most important decision anyone ever makes – the choice of a mate – we dive blindly in with no similar investigation or education regarding the suitability of our 'chosen one.'

Let me say here that at another level, let us call it a 'spiritual level,' I have learned that there are no 'wrong' relationships. This can be more easily understood once we accept that all relationship and life experiences are learning and healing devices, but we can minimize the heartache we need to experience once we have this knowledge. Here are some very basic guidelines for doing just that.

1. Take a hard, critical look at how each of your parents treated you while you were growing up.
Rate each of your parents (or principal caregivers) from 0-10 as you experienced them looking after you, zero being downright lousy and ten being perfect. Feel free to be really critical; no one else will need to see this list. If you have given them each the same mark, even though it may be a low mark, that means your perception of them is pretty equal. This suggests that you have little unconscious gender competition going on within you. Remember, you are half your biological mother and half your biological father at a cellular level. **If you have an unbalanced**

attitude towards them, you will have a similarly unbalanced attitude towards that part of yourself and towards that gender in the world.

It's incredible the havoc this process can cause at a world level when we have leaders of nations wielding immense power and making decisions that – at an unconscious level – are being driven by unhealed childhood wounds.

For example, in my opinion, part of the reason George W. Bush invaded Iraq and started a clearly unprovoked war had its roots in his unconscious desire to prove to his father, George Bush, Sr., that he was as good as him, or even better. His father had gone only as far as Kuwait, failing to go on into Iraq. It appears that his father was a very critical man, that there was alcoholism in the family, and that he used to often compare the young George unfavorably with his brother Jeb. These family issues impact the world more than we realize until we start to examine them.

Similar scenarios also play out in the family law courts where you find judges making outrageous decisions against one parent or the other – when everyone else can see how the decision is so clearly going to be harmful to the children involved.

I was once a witness in a family trial where a mother was trying to get equal access to her children. The father was fighting against this and attempting to limit the children from even seeing their mother. That ought to be the first 'red flag' to any judge – one parent trying to prevent the other parent from having equal access to their children.

In this case, the mother had left what was a lengthy mismatched union. The father would not permit the mother to take her children to visit their grandparents and family members in another country. When the mother complained of this restriction to the judge in the case, the female judge's comment was, "Well I would never let my ex-husband take our daughter on holiday to another country either!"

It is likely that this judge, like many, was making a prejudiced decision based on her own unhealed experiences. There are people in positions of power in every walk of life – including social workers, teachers, psychologists, lawyers, and police officers – who are also, unconsciously, acting out their unhealed childhood experiences to the detriment of those people they are supposed to be serving.

2. If you realize that you're holding on to deep-seated resentments towards one or both of your parents, write a list of your perceptions of each of them and highlight the beliefs that you have taken on as 'fact' as a result of your experiences.

For example, write down "Men are…" and then make a list of all the beliefs you are holding about men. Similarly, write down "Women are…" and then make a list of the beliefs you have about women.

Do a similar exercise with all the major things in your life, such as money, work, etc.

After you've completed your lists, you may be amazed to see how your beliefs in all these areas marry up with your experiences. These words explain this phenomenon:

My beliefs create my reality – what I believe is what I will create. And if I believe that – then I will – and if I don't believe that – then I won't. Which still makes the first statement true – My beliefs create my reality!

When I first saw that written down in *Love Precious Humanity*, a book about the Avatar process' creator, Harry Palmer, it took me a while to get my head around it, but when I finally did, it made perfect sense to me. In simpler terms, it's referred to as 'self-fulfilling prophesies.' The following story is an example of how we create our own reality.

Robert grew up with a very scary and violent mother. She frequently screamed, shouted, hit him and his siblings, and always seemed to blame people for anything that went wrong in her life. Robert became 'the chosen one,' and his mother 'hijacked' him to look after her instead of her looking after Robert. Gradually, he developed a belief that all women were scary and that his job was to look after them and never leave them no matter how badly they may treat him.

This, of course, was obviously untrue – this was only Robert's experience with his own mother. But because he developed such a deep belief in this (perceiving it as fact), when he grew up, he tended to choose violent, needy women and then blamed them when they were only giving him what he was subconsciously asking for!

Now I invite you to examine how your own beliefs, based on your childhood experiences, have played out in your relationships.

3. Once you have uncovered these life-limiting and relationship sabotaging beliefs, rejoice because you can change them!

The wonderful thing about beliefs is that you can change them at any time! They are only repetitive thoughts. Start to notice your language, and most importantly the language of any prospective partner, when discussing the two genders. You will be amazed at the number of people who hold a deep-seated disrespect for one gender or the other, or even both! And then see how it has impacted their life.

A woman I met on my travels was constantly in conflict with the male colleagues she worked with. She had been divorced for some years and made frequent negative references to men in general. One day, I noticed a magnet she used to pin notes to her fridge. The magnet read: "All Men Were Created Equal – Equally USELESS!"

One evening, in a very honest and open discussion with her and a woman friend of mine, she asked us why these men were so unreliable and caused her so many problems. In response to her inquiry, we invited her to look at her beliefs about men and very gently asked about her father. She immediately dropped down into the little wounded girl inside as she burst into tears and explained how her father, who had now been dead for twenty-six years, had sent her off to a boarding school in a foreign country when she was only six years old. She had never forgiven him. Because she had not done her grieving work, healed all the pain, anger, and sadness of that tragic loss, and reached a stage of forgiveness, she kept recreating adult experiences with the men in her life which reflected those unhealed experiences.

Despite being a very attractive and successful woman who openly acknowledged her desire for a fulfilling relationship with a male partner, it didn't happen because of her deep-seated beliefs about men in general.

Do you see how this is so healable once you have the information and willingness to do the work?

4. Make a commitment to eliminate abuse of any kind from your energy field.

This is a deep statement of intention to start loving yourself, which is the first step to finding healthier relationships. Develop a practice of 'zero tolerance' to abuse of any kind – physical, mental, emotional, or sexual, regardless of the person or people involved. Many individuals tolerate incredible bullying and abuse from partners, bosses at work, teachers, parents, siblings, and other family members, which can make it difficult to stop these destructive behaviors. You must be prepared to lose contact with such people for a while. You must be prepared to walk away from your job or relationships to start a new pattern. This is never easy, as people will not want you to change – even if it is better for you – especially if they have been used to having control over you and your life.

Therefore, it's imperative to get support from people you can really trust, preferably people who have done their own healing and have been through similar experiences.

5. Make a written list of the way you DO wish to be treated.
There's something powerful about actually getting it down on paper. If you need to first write how you don't want to be treated simply to clarify how you do want to be treated, that's fine, but as soon as you've clarified what you want, destroy the list of what you don't want.

From that point forward, focus only on how you do want to be treated. This is extremely important because, as the Law of Attraction states, what you focus on is what you'll attract to yourself and get more of in your life.

I often see government warning notices at airports and other public places that say, "Our staff will not tolerate any abusive behavior from the public, and such behavior will be punished by arrest," or words to that effect. How much more effective it would be if the notice said, "Our staff will appreciate respectful, kind, and polite behavior from the public, who deserves the same from our staff."

6. Learn to identify what is acceptable and not acceptable TO YOU, regardless of what others may say.
You might experience some people making comments to you such as, "Oh, I'm only teasing – you're too sensitive." Remember, the only person who has the right to determine what is okay and not okay for you is **you** – the recipient, not the sender!

You may well be very sensitive, but there is no such thing as 'too sensitive.' That message is a very hurtful one that basically says, "You are not okay exactly as you are."

I recently visited my son's school on parents' evening, and one of his tutors kept making the comment that he was too quiet and too reserved. That's not how he is with me or others he feels safe with, and my experience is that most people will only reveal themselves fully when they feel safe and supported. Many teachers and parents do not provide such an environment, and that is often why some very sensitive children will shut down. I made sure I reminded my son that he was not 'too' anything and that he was perfectly okay exactly the way he was, regardless of the tutor's opinion.

Kids need the wisdom and support of people who have undergone their own healing, and it's important that we champion their right to be treated with respect. Too often, some teachers and parents forget that respect is a two-way street regardless of age. Many people work in the fields of education without ever healing their own childhood experiences. This will more often than not result in them projecting those same or similar experiences onto children when it has nothing to do with them. Remember, if you don't 'work it out,' you will 'act it out and pass it on.' Many of us become multi-generational accidents until we take a good, hard look at the family systems from which we came and learn to break free of the unhealthy patterning that was modelled to us.

7. Learn as much as you can about your prospective mate's family.

When possible, observe the relationship between your prospective mate's parents. You may be amazed to find that when you look carefully enough – as these things can be very cleverly camouflaged – it has similar patterns to your own parents' relationship. Listen to how they talk to each other. Are they always respectful, or is there an undercurrent of disrespect?

Watch for gender-discriminating comments such as, "Oh, typical man," or, "Women always do that." Very often, these comments are laughed off as 'only joking,' but rest assured, they often cover a mountain of rage. Who do you think is going to be the recipient of that same kind of rage if you get into a relationship with their child? YOU!

I once attended a workshop run by a facilitator and his wife. They sat side by side during the weekend in front of the group, and he referred to his wife all weekend as 'she' and 'her' instead of by name. I found this disrespectful and thought there was likely to be some old, unhealed 'stuff' this man had not yet attended to.

This hunch of mine was confirmed some weeks later when he sent me an e-mail full of rage and expletives. This was a classic case of his reaction being out of proportion to the event (as discussed earlier) – a sign that something from the past had been triggered. He was teaching forgiveness and yet had not healed sufficiently to prevent him from 'acting out' his anger in a destructive manner on a participant of his workshops.

Of course, I also acknowledge that I was co-creating this; I had to look at my lack of forgiveness of my mother's treatment of my dad. This was a classic case of the gender reversal I mentioned earlier. This man was actually mirroring back to me the behavior I disliked about my mum, not my dad.

To look closely at a prospective mate's family patterns may seem like nit-picking, but the more discerning and choosey you are in the early stage of relationships, the more peaceful your life will be when you eventually make a commitment. I am continually amazed at the number of people who get out of very destructive relationships and then tell me, "You know, I noticed something when I very first met them that concerned me..." Yet, they went ahead with the relationship!

When they ask me why they did that, I explain that the most common reason is that the person's behavior felt **familiar**. It was like a coat that fitted them. As mentioned earlier, the word familiar comes from the word 'family,' and that's why it's so important to go back and view your family of origin and do the healing work.

I want to encourage you to develop an 'I won't settle' attitude in regard to your choices of relationship. You are a beautiful, spiritual being having a human experience in this world, and you deserve to be honored, respected, loved, and cherished. The more you can cement that belief and deepen your sense of self-love, the better your chance of attracting people into your life who will reflect that back to you.

8. Be sure that you and your intended mate have broken the emotional ties with your respective original families.
If you and your intended mate have not broken the emotional ties with your original families (in other words, you are still 'enmeshed' in your original families), it is likely that it will be difficult for you to develop a strong, committed, and fulfilling relationship with each other. Like it or not, you have to 'divorce' your family of origin to be in a position to start a healthy new satellite family of your own with your chosen mate.

This does not mean that you stop loving them or stop visiting them from time to time – not at all. However, it does mean that they are no longer 'number one' in your life – and never will be again. Your new chosen mate is now supposed to be number one.

I am amazed at the number of married people or those in committed relationships who say, "Oh, my mum (or my dad or my brother or sister) is the best friend I have in the world." Wow! What about your partner? – I think to myself.

When I've spoken to 'de-prioritized' partners about this, the majority express a constant feeling of 'not fitting in' to their own family in these situations.

I will discuss the importance of this concept in greater detail later, especially when a couple decides to have children. For the system to remain healthy, the same rule must apply – your relationship with your partner must always be prioritized over your relationship with your kids. I can see some of you bristling already! But give me a chance; I'll examine that in greater detail later.

9. Be vigilant for any signs of addictions in your mate.

What is their pattern of alcohol use? Do they insist on drinking every night? Do they drink very quickly? Do they complain of memory loss or blackouts after a party or session of heavy drinking? Do you notice any subtle, or not so subtle, change of personality after they have had too much to drink? This could even disguise itself as appealing because maybe they become the life and soul of the party when previously they may have been quiet and withdrawn.

Strange though it may seem, these are all early warning signs of problem drinking.

Why would anyone with strong self-love and self-esteem wish to be in a relationship with someone who so obviously does not value themselves?

Same answer as always – because at some level, it feels familiar. So take a good look at your own history. Is there a problem drinker or drug addiction or history of dependency on prescription drugs in your family? Look back at grandparents if necessary, and chances are you will find a clue as to why this behavior feels familiar and, therefore, attractive to you.

Be aware of thinking, Oh well, I'll change him or her once we're together. That is a sure recipe for future misery. The only person you'll ever change in your life is you. And if you spend your time trying to change those around you, you'll end up driving them, and yourself, crazy.

Chapter 7

The Phenomenon of Family History Repeating Itself

When I was studying for a certificate in counselling, we had to create a 'genogram.' This is similar to a family tree, but in addition to recording the names and dates of births, deaths, marriages, etc. of each family member, we were also required to do little biographies on each person. In these brief biographies, we made a note of anything that stood out in the person's life, such as alcohol or drug abuse, criminality, suicide, financial failures, multiple affairs, violent behavior of any kind, unusual career history, and so on.

Once we had each completed our genograms, it was absolutely mind-blowing to see all the repeated patterns. Nearly everyone in the class was shocked at the realization that these patterns were passed on from generation to generation. Very often, the particular situation had been kept a secret from all or some of the family members. It is as though, as long as the information was not in the consciousness of everyone, someone in that family had to recreate a similar situation even though it could well be to their detriment or the detriment of others. Once the situation was brought out into the open, it was as if there was no further need for it to be repeated.

There is an excellent book called *Family Secrets* by John Bradshaw that explains this fascinating phenomenon in greater detail. If any of these examples intrigue you, I recommend that his book, and in fact any book by John Bradshaw, as an excellent read.

Real-Life Example

I was experiencing some difficulty in my relationship with my eldest son, Paul, nothing major, just a kind of 'block' in our communication. He was serving in the British Army and had recently completed his Marine Commando Training. During his time in the military, I had made major life changes and started my inner voyage of self-discovery. I can imagine that it was a real challenge for him to relate to this 'new' dad.

Paul is, and has always been, an extremely gentle and caring young man, and I found it interesting that he joined the army, and even more interesting that he appeared to have an insatiable desire to serve anywhere where there was a war going on. At different times, he expressed his desire to serve in Northern Ireland, Bosnia, Afghanistan, and Iraq. He managed to fulfill some of those desires, but not all of them. I believe in supporting children in whatever their desires are, and so I made no attempt at trying to dissuade him from joining the army, though I wondered at the time what was driving this desire.

When we began experiencing difficulties in our communication, I decided I wanted to do something positive about the situation. I also realized that Paul was not interested at that time in exploring my newfound concepts or entering into dialogue on the subject. In fact, as he explains in the foreword to this book, he let me know he thought that I was talking a lot of crap!

A friend had recommended Constellation Work to me, explaining that it was very successful in releasing past generational memories that may be hindering the life of a family member without them ever knowing the reason. I managed to find such a workshop and signed up for the weekend course. I knew very little about this work, but my intuition was telling me I should attend.

During this work, a trained facilitator invites any member of the group of participants to present some issue that's causing them pain or sadness or anger, an issue they would like to 'clear.' I mentioned the friction with my son, and the facilitator invited me to choose different people from my group to represent my son, my father, my mother, and myself. This facilitator was very intuitive, and as soon as I had chosen the participants, she asked me my father's age when I was born. She mentioned that, judging by my age, he would have probably been away in the military when I was born.

I explained that my father was never in the military, as he had been born with a deformed left leg and was therefore 'not fit' to join the army when the Japanese invaded Malaya, where he was living with my mother and my sister at the time.

The facilitator suddenly gave an indication that she had hit on something and asked me to pick some more participants. She invited me to choose someone to represent the country of Malaya, someone to represent my baby sister, and someone to represent all my father's male friends who had to leave their families to join the army and go off and fight the Japanese.

The people representing my family were grouped together, according to the facilitator's instructions, and the person representing Malaya stood behind them, with the person representing my father's friends in front of them. The group of participants was then invited to focus on their emotions and simply to allow whatever they were feeling to rise to the surface. They were also encouraged to move around wherever they felt inclined. What happened next amazed me. The person representing my father's friends started to slowly walk away from my 'father' and 'mother,' towards the door, and finally walked out of the room. Suddenly, the person representing my father became distressed. He began shaking and looked very angry and then eventually burst into tears, while the woman representing my mother started to cry also. It was very spontaneous and natural. It wasn't long before each of the participants, including me, was crying. Each person slowly approached my 'father' and started to console him and put their arms around him, which helped him to release even more sadness.

The facilitator gently brought this cameo to a close, and we all shared our experiences with the group. What amazed me was that the facilitator was able to hone in on the situation that, on the surface, had no connection to the issue I had presented. Remember, my son had no idea that any of this was going on.

That is one of the most powerful things about this work; the other person does not have to be consciously involved.

After that weekend, when I met up with Paul, there was a distinct improvement in our level of communication, but the greatest shock was still to come to me. About six months later, he started to say that he was tiring of military life despite being chosen as one of the brightest prospects in his unit and having been recommended to attend the Officer's Training School in Sandhurst. A few months later, he quit the army entirely and even turned his back on a security position in Afghanistan; he lost all his desire to be part of any fighting force. In fact, he started a venture with his brother-in-law, helping young people to raise their self-esteem.

Any repressed emotions in past generations can unconsciously be recreated without the person knowing why. In this case, it was probable that my son was carrying the memory of his grandfather's anger, guilt, shame, and sadness at being 'unfit' to represent his country at war.

Imagine the shame my father would have felt at the time, being the only British male left in the community with all these women and their children while all his friends left their families to go and fight.

So my son, who had never known his grandfather (he died seven years before my son was born), felt this inexplicable yearning to 'go to war,' even though it went totally against his peaceful and gentle nature. The Constellation Work symbolically released those repressed feelings of my father's, using a kind of 'surrogate' to express them and have them witnessed by non-shaming faces. When these long-repressed emotions were released, my son no longer carried the urge to go to war.

Chapter 8

Why the Couple Has to Come before the Children

Now, prepare yourself. This topic might really challenge your beliefs.

If a couple has one or both of the essential chemistries missing, and they have children, it is quite common that either one or both of the parents will unwittingly attempt to find the 'connection' that's missing from their partner, with one or more of their children. In this instance, the couple's relationship is sacrificed and the parents' relationship with the children becomes the priority. And there are negative consequences for everyone involved.

It is not my intention to imply that children of various ages do not have needs that require the support of their parents and must occasionally be prioritized over the needs of the parents. The connection that I'm talking about is an energy that runs at a deeper, perhaps unconscious, level.

I'd like to recall for you a real-life incident in order to illustrate what a healthy family looks like.

I was in Cyprus recharging my body with the heat and sun it always craves, and decided to step into one of the roadside bars that come complete with an ever-present giant TV screen to watch the Rugby Union World Cup final between England and South Africa.

As I sat at a table waiting for the game to start, the bar started filling up with fans from both countries and a young woman in her early thirties and her five- or six-year-old son sat down at the table next to me. She had a warm open smile and exuded an air of quiet self-confidence and security.

From the enormous scarf draped around her neck, she clearly supported South Africa. The interaction between the woman and her young son struck me instantly.

As I observed them, the young boy – without any instruction from his mother – took up a seat, not beside her, but in the chair opposite. He then proceeded to take out his coloring books and crayons and enthusiastically create drawings while casually passing an infrequent comment to his mother. She responded to her son's occasional remarks with very obvious kindness and a most caring manner while, at the same time, maintaining a friendly and engaging conversation with her fellow South African supporters and me.

Very soon, her husband arrived from work to join his wife and young son. On entering the bar, he immediately went to his wife first and embraced her warmly with a hug and a gentle kiss. He then did the same with his young son, who responded equally affectionately. What struck me was that all three seemed so calm. There was no overexcitement from the child or any desperation for attention on the arrival of his father. In the same way that he had been comfortable with his mother's lack of constant attention, the boy exhibited a warm and serene acknowledgement that his father had now joined them – and all was well in his little world.

The husband took up his position in the seat beside his wife, opposite the child, and proceeded to join in all the various topics of conversation that ensued.

I recount this scene in such detail because it had a tremendous impact upon me. What amazed me was that the boy lacked any need for constant attention from either of his parents. He had an air of absolute confidence and assuredness about him. I realized that this was probably due to the fact that he knew that Mum and Dad were the king and queen of his little world, and that they were the most important people to each other. The certainty of this knowledge is what gave him the level of security, peace, and tranquility that exuded from him, and I could not help but ponder on how rare it is to witness such qualities in children in today's world.

So many couples make the tragic mistake – albeit completely well-meaning and innocently – of deprioritizing their own relationship and making their children the prime focus of their lives.

Here is a diagram of what I suggest a healthy family system looks like:

Healthy Family System

Mum and Dad are on the same line together, with all four children below them. Variations of these positions will likely create a dysfunction in the system in varying degrees. See the following diagrams, which illustrate just a few possible variations.

Unhealthy Family Systems: Example 1

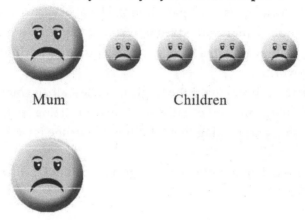

Mum   Children

Dad

Mum aligned with all the kids with Dad 'demoted' like a child. Very often occurs when the couple do not have the chemistry between them, or it has 'waned' over the period of the relationship.

Unhealthy Family Systems: Example 2

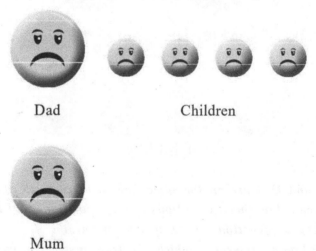

Dad   Children

Mum

Dad aligned with all the kids and Mum 'demoted' to the place of a child. Again, often occurs when the chemistry is not present between the couple.

Unhealthy Family Systems: Example 3

Mum/Dad   Children

Dad/Mum   Children

Mum or Dad aligned with some of the kids with the other parent clearly 'demoted' together with the kids who are not aligned with the other parent.

These diagrams are not meant to imply that one parent will not go somewhere with some of the children while the other parent accompanies the other children on a different outing. With different interests in a family, it is actually very healthy for parents to spend time away from the family and from each other. Time apart indicates that both partners have freedom of choice. Rigid or inflexible attitudes, such as 'where one goes, all must go,' can be very unhealthy. Some of you may recognize that one – "We are the Smith family, and this family always does everything together!"

What the above diagrams are meant to illustrate is something energetic that, believe it or not, children pick up very quickly. I remember speaking with a man who told me that when he was only ten years of age he considered going to his father and asking him why he stayed in a marriage which was clearly so unhappy. His younger sister used to come straight out and ask her parents why and how they ever got together, as they were so clearly incompatible.

Kids always know at a deep level what's going on in their family, and all they want is for their mum and dad to be happy and at peace. When I ask parents what they want for their children, without exception, they answer, "We want them to be happy." When I ask what they think their children want for them, they 'um' and 'err' and need to think about it for a while. They don't immediately get that the kids want exactly the same for them!

So many parents in unhappy marriages or unions claim that they stick together for the sake of the kids. They don't seem to understand that when they do this, they are modelling to their kids that it's best to stay miserable and perhaps even in abusive relationships rather than take the necessary action to change the situation.

This is not to say that unhappy relationships should necessarily end. If the essential chemistries we discussed earlier were present in the beginning of the relationship and both partners are prepared to do healing work, great things can happen. However, if one or both of these chemistries was absent from the start, the union is a mismatch. If nothing is done to address the situation, their kids are likely to repeat the pattern modelled to them by their parents by similarly engaging in a mismatched union. And so the miserable cycle continues.

Chapter 9

Understanding the Destructive Power of Emotional Incest

When Mum and Dad do not have good chemistry, the kids often believe that they must make Mum and/or Dad happy. Often, one of the kids becomes the 'emotional partner,' or the 'caretaker,' of one of the parents – usually the parent who does not seek peers or friends to fill the void that exists in their union with their partner.

The children of these parents can spend the whole of their lives unconsciously attached to one or both of their parents' good opinions of them. They might keep trying to 'make it better,' abandoning their own lives and dreams in the process. When parents rely on their children to fulfill their emotional needs, the relationship reflects an emotional abuse of the child. As mentioned earlier, this situation can be considered a form of 'emotional incest,' because the parent nourishes an inappropriate bond with the child. The effect on the children in these situations is often truly devastating, often inhibiting their ability to form close and lasting intimate relationships when they enter adulthood. *The Emotional Incest Syndrome* by Patricia Love and Jo Robinson and *Silently Seduced* by Dr. Kenneth Adams are two books that explain this phenomenon in more depth.

If you have a sense that you were, and still are, experiencing emotional incest from a parent, you will probably find that it is very challenging to set healthy boundaries in your adult relationships. If you experienced any form of violence from the parent with whom you were emotionally incested, it is highly likely that you will either find yourself tolerating violence and physical abuse or engaging in that behavior and becoming an abuser. In both cases, there is likely to be a sense of confusion as to why you are accepting this type of behavior (if you are the victim) or why you are doing this (if you are the perpetrator). The victim of abuse will often question their right to extricate themselves from the relationship while justifying the behavior of the abusive partner by focusing on and exaggerating their better qualities. "I know they beat me up/ridicule me/put me down, but they are so good and kind a lot of the time," is a comment I hear a lot from victims of domestic violence.

On the other hand, a woman I worked with who was frequently violent towards her husband and children and hated herself for it insisted, "If he ever lays a finger on me it'll be the last thing he ever does." Phrases such as these indicate in both cases that there was a deeply damaging experience in these people's young lives.

A good tool to use if you find yourself in such a situation is to remember that no amount of 'goodness' in you or your mate is a reason to:

a) act out violently; or
b) justify and tolerate violence and abuse.

When one of the partners of a union maintains resentment and bitterness towards the other partner long after a breakup occurs, and fails to move on to other relationships, the bitter partner might cause one or more of the children to become their 'new partner.'

In this case, it is likely that the children are being emotionally incested, and the consequences of such a relationship can have long-lasting and devastating effects on the child's adult relationship life. Very often, even in their adult years, victims of emotional incest remain terrified of displeasing the parents that have become their 'partners,' and they are not even aware of what is happening.

One man I know refused to have any contact with his father for thirty years and admitted to me that the reason was that he and his siblings lived in terror of incurring their mother's displeasure if they were to continue their relationship with their father. So he gave up all contact with his father and became his mother's emotional caretaker, which had disastrous consequences in his own relationship. This kind of emotional incest can be very confusing for the young person, too – while on one level they feel very important and powerful for being elevated to a position above their normal status in the family system, they also sense that it is wrong for them to take that place.

An important thing for parents to keep in mind is that one of their duties as a responsible parent is to gradually prepare their children to leave them. If Mum and Dad are basically not a match, it is likely that they will feel deeply lonely in their relationship. Consequently, it can make it very difficult for the parents to 'let go' of their kids, and then for those children to emotionally individuate from them and start their own healthy, intimate relationships when they enter adulthood.

It needs to be continually reiterated that this is not about kids 'not loving' their parents or parents 'not loving' their kids. It's an energetic thing and, interestingly, the people I speak to who have experienced this enmeshment understand immediately. I often hear them say something like, "I always felt so guilty whatever I did in my life and I could never understand why."

When parents in mismatched unions focus obsessively on the kids because of a lack of connection with the other parent, it's normally because, as adults, they failed to individuate from their family of origin. It's usually the child part of them trying to hold onto their dream of an idealized childhood. Conversely, people who have not yet individuated from their original family might unconsciously choose a mismatched partner so that there is no chance of the partner ever being prioritized over their family of origin and thereby incurring their displeasure.

Couples in mismatched unions often experience enormous denial concerning their situation for one major reason: most of us will normally seek out friends and social circles that resonate and are compatible with our personalities, beliefs, and interests. Such connections can keep us from facing up to the painful truth of our unfulfilling relationship, because we can make the mistake of thinking that our relationships are normal! Let me explain.

If you are in a dysfunctional relationship, you will most likely mix with others who are in similarly dysfunctional situations – so it seems 'normal' to you, and you have no reason to question it. For example, if you are a heavy drinker, it is highly likely that you will hang out with other people who drink to excess. You might even believe that there is something wrong with people who have fun without drinking. You are not forced to examine your own lifestyle and how it might be damaging you and those close to you because you are constantly reassured of the apparent normalcy of your actions.

It is the same with dysfunctional relationships. Because your union seems 'normal' compared to those of the people you know, it is hard to judge whether it is healthy or not. However, there are questions you can ask yourself to see whether your relationship is helpful or hurtful to you and your family.

- Do you find yourself spending more social time with your children than with your spouse/partner or peer group?
- Do you feel more comfortable with your spouse/partner when your children are present?
- Do you use your spouse's/partner's first name or 'nickname' instead of 'mummy/mum' or 'daddy/dad' when referring to them with your children?
- Do you criticize, belittle or in any way make fun of your spouse/partner in the presence of your children?

If you find yourself answering 'yes' to any of these questions it could be that your relationship with your children is being prioritized over that with your spouse/partner. In this case you might find that seeking support from a good family counsellor may help the situation. After all, the most important thing for your family is that it is healthy and happy.

When Mum and Dad are dancing to the same loving tune – physically, mentally, and emotionally – the kids virtually take care of themselves, emotionally. The greatest gift parents can give their children is to love the other parent. Even if they decide they need to dissolve their relationship, it can be done in a space of love and respect. Because children love both of their parents equally, they are likely to internalize any conflict between them, which creates feelings of confusion and misery.

However, when parents that are separating exhibit respect for each other and recognize their responsibility for the split, then children's feelings of love for their parents are no longer embroiled so deeply in the conflict, and they can more easily deal with the change and engage in happy relationships in the future.

Chapter 10

Why the Couple Has to Come before the Children in Second Marriages

If Mum or Dad or both of them are in new relationships, once again the children's deepest desire is still that Mum and Dad will be friends and love each other, even though they may no longer be together – because, remember, the child is made up of 50% Mum and 50% Dad. Their next desire is that Mum and Dad will both be happy. So, it's important to make this next attempt at a relationship your primary relationship – your number-one priority – even though your new mate may not be the biological father or mother of your children.

Often, this over-focusing on the kids when someone remarries or enters a new union comes from a sense of guilt, a parent's belief that somehow they have caused these kids not to be living with their other parent, so the parent spends too much time trying to make up for this.

What seems to be beneficial to everyone in the family is if the biological parent reduces their focus on the children and ensures that they have a good solid relationship with their new mate.

Then the same rule applies: the kids will see Mum and Stepdad, or Dad and Stepmum, sitting on their thrones above the children, together and united, and clearly no one is going to come between them. This allows the children to feel secure and develop in a more healthy manner than they would if they feel that the parent with whom they are residing is constantly in guilt. Also, the children are getting a healthy situation modelled to them, even though it may be with a stepparent, before they embark on their own first relationship.

It is important to understand the incredible power of love. If you really love yourself, it then leads to loving others, and if you can find a way to forgive all and love all, that will eventually lead you to inner peace. It doesn't mean you have to be with someone you don't wish to be with, but you can love them all the same. You can create such a vortex of love that anyone around you will feel safe and comfortable. I have learned that relationships work better when you start ridding yourself of all envy, jealousy, hatred, and start practicing love and forgiveness in all areas of your life.

Love is such a powerful energy; it propels you further than any rocket could shoot you.

Here is a reminder of this power:

The Power of Love
There is no difficulty that enough love will not conquer.

No disease that enough love cannot heal; no door that enough love will not open; no gulf that enough love will not bridge.

No wall that enough love will not throw down; no sin that enough love will not redeem.

It makes no difference how deeply seated may be the trouble, how hopeless the outlook, how great the mistake, a sufficient realization of love will dissolve it all.

If only you could love enough you would be the happiest and most powerful being in the world.
– Emmet Fox, Irish spiritual teacher (1886-1951)

Chapter 11

Dissolving Unworkable Relationships

In this chapter, we will be looking at important tips to follow if the decision has been made, either jointly or by one of the partners, to definitely end the relationship. Because of the very different impact such an ending will have when children are involved, we will examine both scenarios.

When Children Are Involved

If one partner decides to leave the relationship and there are children involved, it is so important that both parties realize that it is not their parting that really damages the kids (although that, of course, is very distressing); it is any bitterness, hatred, resentments, or jealousies between the two parents that cause the greatest damage.

It is crucial for each of the parents to minimize the conflict, and there are many ways this can be done. The first step is to be very conscious of the way in which this devastating news is broken to the children. Obviously, it needs to be done in an age-appropriate manner and without any reference to either party as 'the guilty party.' Even though there are bound to be various levels of anger, hurt, and jealousy if one partner is leaving against the wish of the other, it is essential that none of these are voiced in front of the children.

Involving the children in any information that accuses the other parent, even if infidelity is present or suspected, is never appropriate and will hurt the children dreadfully. If everything possible has been tried to make the relationship work, and it has now been decided that a split is the best course of action, I suggest that getting professional help when dissolving a relationship where children are involved is essential. There are many excellent therapists who specialize in assisting in this process, and I have highlighted these in the resource section.

I am totally against the legal system being involved with divorce and separation, especially when children are involved. Children and parents alike would be far better served if the whole process of divorce, separation, care and control, and issues of financial apportionment were handled by someone in the therapeutic field. Sadly, the majority of legal professionals are trained to try and prove that their client is in the 'right' and the other side is in the 'wrong,' and they make huge amounts of money fighting these useless battles. They are always the only winners, as the parents and children always lose.

The reality is that every breakup is a 50-50 deal. If, at first, you think this is an outrageous statement (because your partner has been unfaithful, for example), I hope that the previous chapters in this little book might assist you in looking at it differently. If couples are willing to get really honest and work with a therapist during their breakup, they may find that they can reach a sense of understanding and peace, which is the greatest gift they can give themselves and their children.

Every child is half their mother and half their father and our parents live within all of us for our whole life – what a thought, eh? So when one parent holds a negative and hurtful attitude towards the other parent, the children from that union unconsciously feel that negativity in themselves.

Consequently, it will drive down their self-esteem because they will feel the bitterness is against a part of them. Keep in mind that anytime you speak badly about the other parent, behave disrespectfully towards them or even harbor hurtful thoughts about them, you are causing serious harm to the children who you purport to love – and, you are also harming yourself.

If you can remember that this is a form of serious child abuse it might assist you in catching yourself when the urge rises to engage in this type of behavior. The solution is to take 100% responsibility for your 50% contribution to the breakup and start to work on yourself. Forgiveness, compassion, and love must be your eventual goal because if you don't get there – you'll repeat your choices in different bodies until you do!

If you feel triggered by what you have just read it could be an indication that you have some work to do in this area! I make no apologies for this because we adults have a responsibility to protect our children from every form of abuse – and make no mistake this behavior is emotional abuse.

If you hold on to all the angst about your ex, and if you have attempted to sour your children's minds about their other parent, eventually, it will come back and haunt you. This practice of intentionally trying to sour a child's mind about their other parent has now been labelled 'Parental Alienation Syndrome,' and there are some excellent books about this deep subject listed in the resource section.

There is incredible, lasting damage this habit can have on innocent children, and it is also likely to impact the way their own relationship history pans out.

Remember to bless everything in your life because everything you bless will end up blessing you back. Similarly, everything you curse will end up cursing you back. It may not happen immediately, and it may not happen from the person or thing you are cursing – but it will come from somewhere in some form.

It has nothing to do with any God punishing you. If your family system ever spoke of 'God punishing you,' please know they didn't realize that God was out playing golf when all this was going on!

It has nothing to do with any God; it's simply what we do to ourselves. This is one of life's great lessons.

When Children Are Not Involved

Although still a traumatic experience, it is clearly not quite as traumatic when couples split and there are no children involved. When this happens, I still recommend ending the relationship with the assistance of a good therapist. It is so crucial to experience proper 'endings' in relationships, because if you do not create a clean and satisfactory 'ending,' it is likely that you will unconsciously take that unfinished business into your next relationship.

Endings are simply an opportunity for each partner to express to the other their feelings about the relationship – both good and not so good.

There are many ways to do this, and even if one of you is not prepared to do this, there are ways that you can achieve an ending without the cooperation of your ex-partner (see the resource section).

Once again, even when there are no children involved, it is still imperative to reach the stage of complete forgiveness, compassion, and love for your ex. This is tough stuff, I know. But I can assure you that if you don't come to an understanding of why you experienced these unfulfilling relationships and take 100% responsibility for your choices, then you are going to unerringly repeat the exercise with a seemingly 'different' person, or spend the rest of your days alone. In this case you might kid yourself that you aren't interested in any relationship, ever again. This usually is a cover-up for your fear that you might experience the pain again.

Chapter 12

The Three Stages of Forgiveness in Relationships

Stage 1: They/he/she did this to me, and I forgive them. (So now I assume a 'superior' position to the other which does not bring peace.)

Stage 2: They/he/she didn't do it *to* me, but *for* me – for my own lessons and growth. (This creates a somewhat more peaceful experience, however, there is still a sense that the other is responsible for my feelings – so therefore I am still feeling somewhat of a 'victim.')

Stage 3: They/he/she didn't actually do anything to cause me discomfort, but it was my interpretation of what seemed to happen which disturbed my peace. None of it really happened; I am the creator of my own experiences because my thoughts and beliefs are so powerful and these are projected outward so that my life becomes an expression of these.

Stage 1

I have learned, from studying and, more importantly, practicing the principles of *A Course in Miracles* for nearly two decades, that true forgiveness is a process that has to be learned. My own experience is that these three important stages of forgiveness mentioned above were a crucial part of my healing. It was so important that I passed through and experienced the first two stages before jumping into the third and final stage.

Once I made the decision that I wanted to find a better way of living and being in the world, I asked my intuition (inner teacher, what ACIM calls The Holy Spirit), to show me my next step. As always, when we ask we always receive, but not always in the way we might have envisaged.

I was attending a weekend convention of Alcoholics Anonymous. It was the evening time with dance, music and fun. A woman, a fellow AA member, approached me and invited me to dance. My ego fear swamped me at the thought. "Oh thanks, but I'm not feeling well," I lied. Then the shame of being untruthful engulfed me and I excused myself and slunk off to my bedroom at the retreat center.

I felt so disgusted with myself and lay on my bed, staring up at the ceiling crying out, "Why can I not get on a dance floor without alcohol in me? Somebody up there please help me."

The following morning I attended college where I was studying for a Diploma in Therapeutic Counselling when one of my peer group excitedly approached me brandishing a thin book exclaiming, "John, you must read this book. It's truly amazing."

The title of the book was *Healing the Child Within* by Charles Whitfield. Now, at this stage of my journey I had not yet heard of the term 'Inner Child' or 'Child Within,' as the author called it. But as soon as my friend showed me the book, my inner teacher, the voice within which always knows what is best for me, told me this was for me. I had not yet come in contact with ACIM at this time so was unfamiliar with the term 'Holy Spirit' or 'Voice from God' so I just called this feeling my 'Zing.' When my 'Zing' would go off for any reason it was my signal to pay close attention!

So I read the book from cover to cover in very quick time. It was only a thin book and I liked that. As soon as I finished the book I realized that this book was the answer to my plea, "Why can I not get on a dance floor without alcohol in me?" I now understood that I had this little boy inside me who was riddled with shame about his body and had no desire to get up and prance around a dance floor for everyone to laugh at me! See how vicious my ego was? ACIM explains, "The ego is capable of suspiciousness at best and viciousness at worst." T-9.VII

Regardless of this ego attack I was now determined to do whatever I was guided to do to heal this inner child of mine. I had had enough of the shame and guilt which I was carrying and I asked again, "Show me the very best course in order to accomplish this healing." No sooner had I put this request out into the ether, once again, I received the answer.

I was glancing through a magazine entitled *South East London Connection* and a page on the right-hand side jumped out at me. It was advertising a course entitled, in those days, "The Hoffman Quadrinity Process" (now simply "The Hoffman Process"). What grabbed my attention were two things. Firstly there was an endorsement from John Bradshaw which praised the efficacy of this course in healing the wounds of childhood and getting back in touch with our True selves.

What hit me was the fact that I was in the process of starting a book of John Bradshaw's entitled *Healing the Shame That Binds You*. So I saw this as a 'message' to confirm that this Hoffman course was, indeed, for me.

The second thing which jumped out at me was that the head office of The Hoffman Institute in the UK was in the tranquil town of Arundel on the south coast of Sussex. My deep connection with this town was that, as a young child, I would run away from my then crazy alcoholic mother during school holidays or weekends and take refuge in the beautiful grounds of Arundel Castle. I found great respite just by sitting quietly alone and enjoying the peace which was absent in my family home.

Those two 'signs' were sufficient for me. I absolutely knew that this course was for me. Despite knowing nothing about the course or anyone who had experienced the course, I telephoned the Institute immediately to enquire when their next course was running. The person who answered the phone was the co-founder of The Hoffman Institute in the UK, Tim Laurence. He and Serena, his wife at the time, had both experienced the course in North America and Canada and had brought this work to the UK.

Tim was quite shocked when I asked him to take my credit card details without knowing a thing about the course. He recommended that I first speak with a former participant who might answer any questions I might have. However, I was unmoved. My inner guide had given me all the confirmation I needed. So I enrolled immediately for the very next course.

I went into this work twenty years after my mother had passed away and twenty-nine years after my father had passed away. At the time, I was still holding a belief that my mother was the 'devil' and my father was the 'saint.'

I had made a classic 'separation' of my parents and blamed my alcoholic mother for everything. Consequently, I had an acute imbalance of my own inner male and female sides, which then manifested in my outer world. I held a belief that all women were cruel and unloving and that they were never present. I also had a belief that men were supposed to grin and bear everything and never get angry; thus, I developed a classic 'victim' mentality.

During this process work, which was an intensive seven days, I was able to go back and take an in-depth look at my childhood. I was given the opportunity to actually feel and express all the anger, hurt, and deep sadness of my seemingly lost childhood.

I was then given an opportunity to examine, equally carefully, the childhoods of both of my parents and feel the same pain they must have experienced growing up. After these incredibly tough seven days, I found a place of total acceptance and self-love; and forgiveness and compassion for both of my parents. The most powerful experience, though, was this feeling of total balance between them. I experienced them both as equal, with one not a fraction better or worse than the other.

This had an amazingly powerful positive effect on my life. It was only the start of my healing, but at least I no longer felt any male/female difference at a deep level and had healed this imbalance within me. Gradually, I noticed I no longer made any inappropriate gender difference comments like, "Women do this," or, "Men do that," and became increasingly sensitive to generalizations of that type from others. I had healed most of my male/female separation issues.

Stage 2

I came across a book called *Radical Forgiveness* by Colin Tipping, and I decided to undertake his Radical Forgiveness workshop in Atlanta, Georgia.

It had many of the same concepts of The Hoffman Process and was not nearly as intense – it only ran over a weekend. The workshop deepened my understanding of the theory that everything happens in my life for my own growth and learning. I was given some excellent worksheets that helped to remind me of that basic precept when I found myself going into 'blame.'

Even though I found the workshop to be very helpful, I knew there was still something more I needed to find – as I still had this sense of 'seeking' for something.

Stage 3

I like to call this stage of forgiveness 'Quantum Forgiveness' because it requires a quantum leap in understanding the forgiveness process. This teaching came in the form of a spiritual self-study volume known as *A Course in Miracles* (ACIM). This masterpiece first came into my life as early as 1999 when I was at college studying Therapeutic Counselling. I had been doing some co-counselling homework with a fellow classmate, and as I left her house I saw the famous, thick, blue book on a table near her front door. "Oh, that looks interesting. I'd love to learn how to do miracles!" my ego commented. My colleague didn't say much, but it was enough for me to get the book.

When it arrived, I had a brief look at the contents. It looked a lot like a Bible with its wafer-thin pages and heavy text. I was more intrigued at how the book had come about, which was briefly explained in the first pages.

Anyway, I kept dipping into the book and attending various ACIM study groups but never took it too seriously. I was aware that most of the authors whom I admired in the self-help and spiritual field of writing seemed to be students of ACIM and made the connection that there must be something in this stuff, but it all seemed too heavy to me and often sounded like double Dutch.

Interestingly, despite my habit of always passing any books I had bought onto others, I never gave this book away, and it went with me on all my travels to different parts of the world.

In 2003, I received an e-mail newsletter from Dr. Wayne Dyer recommending a new book called *The Disappearance of the Universe* by Gary Renard.

I was totally enthralled by the book and greatly relieved to understand the explanations it offered for the real meaning of ACIM. From that day forward, I became a committed student of ACIM; I completed all the *Text*, the 365 lessons of the *Workbook*, and the *Manual for Teachers*, and I continue to reread the book on a daily basis.

It may be that ACIM is not for everyone, and it is not my intention to guide people to any one particular model of healing. There are many ways to do this work of quantum forgiveness and, as ever, I encourage you to find what works best for you.

I would like to express my belief in the importance of doing 'original pain' work before embarking on higher spiritual practices. I have found that when the deep grief work is not undertaken and someone gets involved with high spiritual practices and theories, the old, unprocessed anger can seep out in very subtle and sometimes not so subtle ways.

People who fail to do this type of work are sometimes referred to as 'unhealed healers.' I like the phrases, 'having a spiritual bypass' or 'spiritual leapfrogging,' as they so aptly describe the process of missing out on the lower-self healing. This sometimes happens with sponsors, therapists or workshop leaders who unconsciously act out these unhealed processes from positions of perceived 'power' onto the people they are supposed to be helping. For this reason, I provide tips on choosing therapists and workshops in the resource section.

Conclusion

One of the major lessons I had to learn both in relationships and in life in general is that I can never control or change another person. Many people spend their entire lives trying to control everyone and everything around them, but we cannot control anyone but ourselves.

I would like to emphasize that nothing in these pages is intended to be a criticism or condemnation of any person or group of people. One thing I am absolutely convinced of after many, many years of serious self-examination and introspection is that everyone, without exception, is doing what they believe is right with the understanding they have. They are doing the best they can with the 'tools' they've got. I no longer believe in 'bad people' but only in 'hurt people.' And one thing is sure, 'hurt people' – hurt people. If not others, then themselves and frequently both.

One of the reasons so many of us have such a tough time removing ourselves from, or refusing to accept, behavior or attitudes we find offensive, both in our personal relationships and at work, has its roots in our early home life and our traditional educational models.

I know that there are many wonderful schools in the world that honor the wishes of the child in choosing what they want to learn and when they want to learn. I'm not talking about those. I am referring to the more common type of school where they have to follow the government decreed course of study.

In this system, if a child consistently and continuously is forced to do and study what they do not enjoy, and is deprived of doing that which the child does enjoy, new neural pathways are produced in the brain that send the message that the person has to do what may feel uncomfortable or displeasing to them.

I would suggest that these deeply ingrained 'compliance' patterns kick in when that person is experiencing abuse of any kind, and I would contend that this is the reason why so many people are prepared to settle for unfulfilling relationships and jobs.

The latest research in brain neuroplasticity has shown that the brain continues to build these new neural pathways throughout our whole life. The positive side of this finding is that it is possible to start producing new pathways that give the message that what the person is experiencing is not okay, and so they can start setting boundaries.

I have an unshakable belief in the innate goodness within the essence of all humanity, and I would suggest that the cruelty and pain we inflict on each other and ourselves has its roots in self-hatred and intense guilt.

If that is the case, then surely the remedy must be self-love and letting go of guilt and realizing our innate innocence. That is what I am recommending as one sure way of improving your relationship choices.

As I have reiterated earlier, this little book is only intended as an introduction to the complex subject of relationships. My hope is that you will have found sufficient information within these pages to make a sincere commitment to yourself to do whatever it takes to ensure that, whether you are already in or not yet in a committed intimate relationship, you will not settle for less than is your birthright and that which you so richly deserve – a deeply and mutually fulfilling union, full of joy, fun, happiness, healing, friendship, and great sex!

Yes, believe it or not, great sex is your birthright too. A safe and sacred place where you can explore your own and each other's bodies with a sense of total innocence as you also heal any old shame and guilt that may have been unwittingly passed down to you by your family and/or cultural or religious belief system. And remember this exploration can be ageless – great sex has nothing to do with your age! (See www.innocentsex. org.)

Intimate relationships can also be a place where you can find a way to learn to safely disagree with each other without being disagreeable. In many family systems, when members fall out or disagree over something, they end up not speaking for months and even years. No one has modelled to them how to disagree and still stay friends.

The research section has been carefully constructed for you to explore in greater depth anything you feel drawn to. I can guarantee you that, unless specifically mentioned to the contrary, I have personally read every book and attended every workshop and therapist to which and to whom I refer in these pages.

I would also like to add that if the word 'God' is niggling you, please know that it used to do the same to me until I searched for another idea of God – not the angry, punishing man in the sky I'd been taught about as a child. This is a loving, kind, and totally forgiving God who has been with me and *a part* of me all my life – not *apart* from me as I had been taught.

Whatever your experience of the word God has been, allow me to share the words of the great Sufi poet Hafiz, who said, "In the end you only have two choices – you either come to God dressed for dancing or you get wheeled into God's ward on a stretcher." I have found that to be so true. Another thing you could try, if you have a block with the word God, is to simply substitute the word Love – I find it is the same thing!

Appendix

Forgiveness offers everything I want

A Course in Miracles from Lesson 122.

1. What could you want that forgiveness cannot give? Do you want peace? Forgiveness offers it. Do you want happiness, a quiet mind, a certainty of purpose, and a sense of worth and beauty that transcends the world? Do you want care and safety, and the warmth of pure protection always? Do you want a quietness that cannot be disturbed, a gentleness that never can be hurt, a deep abiding comfort, and a rest so perfect it can never be upset?

2. All this forgiveness offers you, and more. It sparkles on your eyes as you awake, and gives you joy with which to meet the day. It soothes your forehead while you sleep, and rests upon your eyelids so you see no dreams of fear and evil, malice and attack. And when you wake again, it offers you another day of happiness and peace. All this forgiveness offers you, and more.

20 Tips to Creating Healthy Relationships

1. Examine your childhood experiences and your parents' and grandparents' (where possible) relationship stories. Find out as much as you can about your family tree in respect to their relationships.

2. Make a list of all the beliefs you may have formed about men and women as a result of these family experiences which negatively impacted any of your relationships. Become willing to change these negative beliefs. Remember that a belief is only a thought you keep thinking. So if you desire to have a different belief, then just make a commitment to change your habitual thought pattern.

3. Make a commitment to change any beliefs that might be blocking your ability to have healthy relationships.

4. Make a commitment to start your own healing journey in whatever way works best for you. Remember, every one of us has experienced 'stuff' – just in varying degrees.

5. Understand this work is not about blaming parents, family members, or anyone else, but it is about recognizing where unhealthy patterns have come from and breaking this chain.

6. Make a commitment to practice a 'zero tolerance' attitude towards abuse, especially towards yourself. Remember that you may have grown up with parents who had very deep emotional and personality disorders, which are not your responsibility and which are not possible for you to heal.

7. If you are with someone who slaps, hits, screams, shouts, throws objects, pushes, pokes, or in any way violates your body or mind, it is likely that you are dealing with one of these personality disorders. These are serious and will not simply go away.

8. If there are children involved, then they are witnessing this, and if anyone is a witness to any kind of abuse, they are also being abused. So talk to someone you really trust, get a support system in place, and then if you decide you wish to leave – get out of there as fast as you can. People with serious disorders can become very dangerous when they experience someone 'abandoning' them. So do get good support first.

9. Be careful to watch out for any addictive habits you may have or any prospective partner may have. Alcohol, drugs, prescribed medication, work, and sexual compulsivity are some of the most common addictions. We are all addicted to something – even sugar – but we are not all addicts! So make sure that you and your prospective mate are aware

of any destructive habits, and make a commitment to deal with yours.

10. Make sure that you have the two basic chemistries with your mate before you make a commitment. Remember that sexual chemistry and best friend chemistry must both be present if your relationship is to stand a chance of going the distance and being mutually fulfilling.

11. Discuss your ideas of partnership and make agreements about children, shared responsibilities, finances, and other vital topics before you make a commitment. Are your beliefs about relationships in tune with each other? Do you both really want to have children? If one does and the other doesn't, no need to go any further and make a doomed commitment.

12. Make sure that your prospective partner understands the principles of relationships and is prepared to go on this healing journey with you. If they don't agree, chances are you'll end up getting continually 'blamed' for their uncomfortable feelings.

13. Make a commitment to deepening your sense of self-love. The more you can love yourself unconditionally, the greater are the chances of you attracting, and keeping, a loving and healthy mate.

14. Make a list of everything you have ever done and a list of what others have done to you, of which you are ashamed or about which you feel any twinge of anger and/or guilt. No one needs to see the list, but make it just the same.

15. Then alongside each of these things, write the words "and I forgive myself and them." If there is someone whom you really trust – and that is the most important piece – that you would feel comfortable sharing the list with, ask them if they will agree to have you read it to them.

16. If you are able to do this, read the list to them and let all the emotions that surface just flow out. When you have

finished, you can have a little ceremony or ritual where you burn the list and thereby transmute the energy. This is very powerful.

17. If you have no one whom you feel comfortable enough to share this with, then simply have a little ceremony yourself and burn the list when you have finished. You can always 'imagine' certain people being with you.

18. Avoid spending unnecessary time with anyone who tries to put you down, criticizes you, or tries to put guilt onto you. Remember that people who do this feel bad about themselves and therefore try to push others down in order to try and make themselves feel better. Some people join the teaching professions, the police, the military, and other 'power' professions so that they can legitimize their rage on those in a subordinate position. I encourage you to be aware of this and take necessary action to report such abuse if you encounter it.

19. Be prepared to report such inappropriate behavior to responsible authorities. Many people who have been abused as children by parents and/or authority figures have been conditioned to keep silent about any abuse. 'Don't ever wash your dirty linen in public' is a favorite message used by abusive family systems. Another one is, 'Blood is thicker than water – you can't trust those who are not from the same blood.' These are very unhealthy and controlling messages ensuring that you never speak about the abuse to outsiders – and so it keeps on happening.

20. When you have done your 'original pain' work, make a commitment to start practicing forgiveness in your life, remembering that forgiveness has to be learned and is a state of mind and heart. It does not mean that you have to hang around with the people you are forgiving – even if they are family members.

Resources

There is a lot to choose from here. I encourage you to first notice what appeals to your intuition, and then carry out your due diligence in whatever way feels right for you before making your choices.

Since starting this work, I have found that when I quiet my mind and consciously ask my intuition to guide me, I always receive direction.

Sometimes it takes the form of someone telling me about a book they've read or a course they've experienced. Though it takes many forms, the guidance always shows up.

I have included some books, courses, and trainings that I have not personally experienced but can recommend from other trusted sources; I have marked these with an asterisk. Clearly there may be other such therapists in your geographical area who will have similar abilities and integrity. I do encourage you, however, to really do your homework when choosing a therapist, counsellor, or coach. I recommend inquiring about not only their professional qualifications and their supervisory support but also what courses they themselves have undertaken for their own healing.

I once visited an EMDR therapist when this modality was still relatively new in the UK. She asked about my belief system, and I told her that I believed we all had the power to heal anything and that we shared the same potential as Jesus as healers. I also explained that I felt the mind was the root cause of all illness.

The therapist listened to me and then commented, "Okay, so what I think we are dealing with here is a case of disassociation and delusions of grandeur." I paid my money for the session, forgave us both and took leave immediately.

Be sure you find someone with whom you feel safe and connected. Always be prepared to walk away from a therapist, counsellor, coach or sponsor if it does not feel right for you. They are not bad people, but as in every other field of expertise, there are those who have different levels of ability and integrity than others. The most important aspect of any therapist is the level of their own healing they have undertaken. It is impossible for a therapist/coach/sponsor to help anyone beyond a stage where they have reached in their own healing.

All healing is a never-ending journey and all therapy is a two-way healing process – you are also facilitating healing in your therapist so avoid putting them on a pedestal.

Finally, please let go of any belief you may have held that you ever had any 'failed' relationships – regardless of how others may perceive them.

There is no such thing as a 'failed' relationship. Every person who has ever come into your life has done so for a mutual learning experience. Each of you has brought something the other needs to learn. Sometimes that lesson could be for you to stand up for yourself, set boundaries and walk away from that which doesn't work for you. So even in that situation your partner has been a great teacher to you and therefore deserves your gratitude.

Whatever your individual experiences may have been – I encourage you to keep your belief in FORGIVENESS, COMPASSION AND LOVE. Let those three things be your guide as you journey through life.

I trust that you will have found this little book of help – it may even have triggered some emotions for you. If that is the case I encourage you to stay with those feelings; know that you are safe and that you are more than your feelings. Someone once commented that this kind of stuff takes you out of your misery and into your pain! – that is always a sign that your healing is starting.

Thank you for sharing your precious time with me. I wish you great healing, peaceful, and loving relationships in every area of your life and I look forward to meeting you somewhere, sometime in this amazing University of life.

With love
John Campbell

Resource List

Emotional, family of origin, and addiction healing books

Adult Children of Parental Alienation Syndrome: Breaking the Ties That Bind by Amy J.L. Baker

Beyond Codependency by Melody Beattie

Beyond the Twelve Steps: Roadmap to a New Life by Lynn Grabhorn

Blessed Are the Addicts by John A. Martin

Codependent No More by Melody Beattie

Dibs in Search of Self by Virginia Axline

Emotional Incest Syndrome: What to Do When a Parent's Love Rules Your Life by Patricia Love and Jo Robinson

Families and How To Survive Them by John Cleese and Robin Skynner

Family Secrets by John Bradshaw

Fathers-To-Be Handbook by Patrick Houser

For Your Own Good by Alice Miller

Healing the Child Within: Discovery and Recovery for Adult Children of Dysfunctional Families by Charles L. Whitfield

Healing the Shame That Binds You by John Bradshaw

I Hate You – Don't Leave Me: Understanding the Borderline Personality by J. Kreisman and Hal Straus

Jonathan Livingston Seagull (Allegory) by Richard Bach

On Becoming a Person by Carl Rogers

Overcoming Addiction by Corinne Sweet

Ponder on This by Alice Miller

Silently Seduced by Dr. Kenneth Adams

Stop Walking on Eggshells: Taking Your Life Back When Someone You Care About Has Borderline Personality Disorder by Paul T. Mason and Randi Kreger

The Big Book of Alcoholics Anonymous by Alcoholics Anonymous

The Drama of Being a Child by Alice Miller
The Family: A New Way of Creating Solid Self-Esteem by John Bradshaw
The Hoffman Process by Tim Laurence
The Journey by Brandon Bays
The Language of Letting Go by Melody Beattie
The Three Stages of Healing by Carolyn Myss
They F*** You Up: How to Survive Family Life by Oliver James
Toxic Parents by Dr. Susan Forward
Understanding the Borderline Mother: Helping Her Children Transcend the Intense, Unpredictable and Volatile Relationship by Christine Lawson
You Can Change Your Life: A Future Different from Your Past with The Hoffman Process by Tim Laurence
You Can Heal Your Life by Louise L. Hay

Groups, venues, and therapeutic techniques

Alcoholics Anonymous Meetings (in UK)
+44845 769 7555
www.alcoholics-anonymous.org.uk

Alcoholics Anonymous World Services
+1 212 870 3400
www.aa.org

Borderline Personality Disorder Resource*
www.bpdcentral.com
www.bpdworld.org

Broadway Lodge Treatment Centre for Addictive Disorders
+441934 812319
www.broadwaylodge.org.uk

Clearmind International
www.clearmind.com

EMDR (Brilliant technique for dealing with acute traumas)
www.emdr.com

Emotional Freedom Technique – World Center For EFT
www.emofree.com

Fathers-To-Be – Expectant Fathers – Patrick Houser
& Elmer Postle
+441892890614
www.fatherstobe.org

Hypnotherapy – The Hypnotherapy Association
+441257262124
www.thehypnotherapyassociation.co.uk

Sabine Young*
+44207 88762439
www.relationshiptherapylondon.co.uk

SOURCE Process and Breathwork – Binnie Dansby
+441892890614
www.binniedansby.com

The Hoffman Institute International Directory
www.hoffmaninstitute.com

The Hoffman Institute UK (The Hoffman Process)
+441903889990
www.hoffmaninstitute.co.uk

The Journey Work – Brandon Bays
+441656890400
www.thejourney.com

The NLP Academy – Neuro Linguistic Programming
+442086869952
www.nlpacademy.co.uk

The Star Process
+1 888 857 7827
www.starfound.org

Physical healing and nutrition books

Cancer – Why We're Still Dying to Know the Truth by Phillip Day
Heal Your Body by Louise L. Hay
Messages from Water by Dr. Masaru Emoto
Sanctuary: The Path To Consciousness by Stephen Lewis and
Evan Slawson
*The Body Talk System: The Missing Link to Optimum Health** by
Dr. John Veltheim
The Journey by Brandon Bays
We Want to Live by Aajonus Vonderplanitz
World Without Aids by Phillip Day
*Your Body Speaks Your Mind: Understanding the Link between
Your Emotions and Your Illness* by Debbie Shapiro

Therapeutic techniques
Acupuncture
www.acupuncture.com

AIM Program
https://aimprogram.com

Breathwork
www.breathe-mag.co.uk

Colon Therapy
www.colonic-association.org

Emotional Freedom Technique (EFT)
www.emofree.com

Eye Movement Desensitization &
Reprocessing (EMDR)
www.emdr.com

IBA Global Healing
www.bodytalksystem.com

Massage Naturopathy (UK)
www.naturopaths.org.uk

Naturopathy (USA)
www.naturopathic.org

Rolfing
www.rolfing.org

The Alexander Technique
www.alexandertechnique.com

The Journey Work – Brandon Bays
+441656890400
www.thejourney.com

Relationships books

22 Boyfriends to Happiness: My Story and the Seven Secrets on How to Find True Love by Catherine Buchan

Getting the Love You Want: A Guide for Couples by Harville Hendrix

The New Couple: Why the Old Rules Don't Work and What Does by Maurice Taylor and Seana McGee

What's the State of Your Union: Instant Relationship Self-Diagnosis by Seana McGee and Maurice Taylor

Groups, workshops, therapists, and techniques

Imago Relationships International

+1212 240 7433

https://imagorelationships.org/

Sabine Young*

+44207 88762439

www.relationshiptherapylondon.co.uk

Sexual healing books

*Healing Love Through the Tao: Cultivating Female Sexual Energy** by Mantak Chia

Innocent Sex: A Path from Guilt to Freedom by Dr. Anne & John Campbell

Slow Sex by Diana Richardson

*Taoist Secrets of Love: Cultivating Male Sexual Energy** by Mantak Chia; Michael Winn

The Art of Sexual Ecstasy: The Path of Sacred Sexuality for Western Lovers by Margo Anand

The Sexual Healing Journey: A Guide For Survivors of Sexual Abuse by Wendy Maltz

Education and parenting books

*Beyond Discipline: From Compliance to Community** by Alfie Kohn

Fathers-To-Be by Patrick Houser

Messages from Water by Dr. Masaru Emoto

No Contest: The Case Against Competition by Alfie Kohn

Punished By Rewards: The Trouble with Gold Stars, Incentive Plans, A's, Praise, and Other Bribes by Alfie Kohn

The Care and Feeding of Indigo Children by Dr. Doreen Virtue

The Case Against Standardized Testing: Raising the Scores, Ruining the Schools by Alfie Kohn

The Crystal Children by Dr. Doreen Virtue

The Homework Myth: Why Our Kids Get Too Much of a Bad Thing by Alfie Kohn

The Indigo Children: The New Kids Have Arrived by Lee Carroll and Jan Tober

The Schools Our Children Deserve: Moving Beyond Traditional Classrooms and "Tougher Standards" by Alfie Kohn

Unconditional Parenting: Moving from Rewards and Punishment to Love and Reasoning by Alfie Kohn

Vital Impressions: The KPM Approach to Children by Dr. Gary Borich

*What Does It Mean to Be Well Educated? More Essays on Standards, Grading, and Other Follies** by Alfie Kohn

What to Look for in a Classroom... and Other Essays by Alfie Kohn

*You Know What They Say... The Truth About Popular Beliefs** by Alfie Kohn

Child centered schools, groups, and workshops

Sri Atmananda Memorial School, Austin, Texas, USA

www.samschool.org

Student Assistance Training
International – Cheryl Watkins
+16028677851
www.cwsap.com

Separation and divorce books

Adult Children of Parental Alienation Syndrome: Breaking the Ties that Bind by Amy J.L. Baker
Children Held Hostage: Dealing With Programmed and Brainwashed Children by Dr. Stanley S. Clawar
Divorce Poison: Protecting the Parent-Child Bond from a Vindictive Ex by Richard Warshak
Spiritual Divorce by Debbie Ford
The Parental Alienation Syndrome by Dr. Richard Gardner

Groups, workshops, and therapists

Imago Relationships International
+1212 240 7433
https://imagorelationships.org/

Sabine Young*
+44207 88762439
www.relationshiptherapylondon.co.uk

Spiritual Divorce Coaching*
www.debbieford.com

Mind power and personality books

As A Man Thinketh by James Allen (www.asamanthinketh.net)
Awaken the Giant Within by Anthony Robbins
Feel the Fear and Do It Anyway by Susan Jeffers
Messages from Water by Dr. Masaru Emoto (www.hado.net)
Power vs. Force by David R. Hawkins

The Color Code: A New Way To See Yourself, Your Relationships and Life by Taylor Hartman
The Enneagram: Understanding Yourself and the Others In Your Life by Helen Palmer
The Power of Your Subconscious Mind by Joseph Murphy

Groups and workshops
Hypnotherapy
+442073851166
www.hypnotherapytraininginstitute.org

Neuro Linguistic Programming
www.nlpacademy.co.uk

The Color Code
www.colorcode.com

The Enneagram Institute
+18456879878
www.enneagraminstitute.com

Creating abundance in all areas of your life books
A Course In Miracles from Foundation For Inner Peace
As A Man Thinketh by James Allen
Ask and It Is Given by Esther Hicks and Jerry Hicks
Life Was Never Meant to Be a Struggle by Stuart Wilde
Manifest Your Destiny by Dr. Wayne Dyer
Miracles by Stuart Wilde
Money is Love by Barbara Wilder
Open Your Mind to Prosperity by Catherine Ponder
Open Your Mind to Receive by Catherine Ponder
The Abundance Book by John Randolph Price
The Dynamic Laws of Prosperity by Catherine Ponder

The Game of Life and How To Play It by Florence Scovel Shinn
The Little Money Bible by Stuart Wilde
The Prospering Power of Love by Catherine Ponder
The Seven Spiritual Laws of Success by Deepak Chopra
The Trick to Money is Having Some! by Stuart Wilde
Think and Grow Rich by Napoleon Hill
You Can Heal Your Life by Louise L. Hay

Groups, venues, and workshops
Abraham-Hicks Productions
www.abraham-hicks.com

Money Is Love
+17208415820
www.barbarawilder.com

Stuart Wilde
www.stuartwilde.com

The Journey
+441656890400
www.thejourney.com

Meditation and spiritual techniques
Transcendental Meditation
+44169551213
www.tm.org

Vipassana 10 Day Silent Meditation Retreats
www.dhamma.org

Yoga
www.yoga.co.uk

Forgiveness, spiritual, and metaphysical work books

A Course In Miracles from Foundation For Inner Peace

A Course In Miracles Made Easy by Alan Cohen

A Little Book of Forgiveness: Challenges & Meditations for Anyone With Something to Forgive by D. Patrick Miller

A Return to Love by Marianne Williamson

Absence from Felicity by Dr. Kenneth Wapnick

Are You As Happy As Your Dog? by Alan Cohen

Conversations With God (1, 2 & 3) by Neale Donald Walsch

Crystal Therapy – How To Heal and Empower Your Life with Crystal Energy by Doreen Virtue & Judith Lukomski

Forgiveness: The Greatest Healer of All by Dr. Gerald G. Jampolsky

Journey Without Distance by Robert Skutch

Living with Miracles: A Common Sense Guide to A Course In Miracles by D. Patrick Miller

Love Has Forgotten No One by Gary Renard

Love Without Conditions by Paul Ferrini

Out on a Limb by Shirley MacLaine

Radical Forgiveness by Colin Tipping

The Alchemist (Allegory) by Paulo Coelho

The Awakener by Sandy Stevenson

The Celestine Prophecy (Allegory) by James Redfield

The Dark Side of the Light Chasers by Debbie Ford

The Disappearance of the Universe by Gary Renard

The Dragon Doesn't Live Here Anymore by Alan Cohen

The Healing of America by Marianne Williamson

The Lightworker's Way by Doreen Virtue

The Lost Mode of Prayer by Gregg Braden

The Prophet by Kahlil Gibran

Whispering Winds of Change by Stuart Wilde

Why Your Life Sucks: And What You Can Do About It by Alan Cohen

Your Immortal Reality by Gary Renard
Zero Limits by Joe Vitale & Dr. Ihaleakala Hew Len

Groups, venues, and workshops
A Course in Miracles
www.acim.org

Angel Therapy
www.angeltherapy.com

Attitudinal Healing International
www.ahinternational.org

Avatar
www.avatarepc.com

Clearmind International
www.clearmind.com

Corstone Center*
www.corstone.org

Crystal Friends
www.crystalfriends.com

Educo Seminars – Dr. Tony Quinn
www.educoworld.com

Foundation for A Course in Miracles*
www.facim.org

Gary Renard
www.garyrenard.com

Ho'oponopono
www.hooponopono.org

Radical Forgiveness
www.radicalforgiveness.org

The Hoffman Process
www.hoffmaninstitute.com

Zero Limits – Joe Vitale & Dr. Ihaleakala Hew Len
www.zerolimits.info

*Anything marked * indicates that I have not read the book, attended the workshop or personally experienced the therapist/counsellor or coach, but that I have a knowledge of the contents/workshop or person and that I feel happy to recommend them.*

A RELATIONSHIP PRAYER TO BEGIN EVERY DAY

(This can be used for any relationship)

A PRAYER FOR RELATIONSHIPS

"Beloved Mother/Father God, I thank you for the gift that (NAME) is in my life. I know that You have sent me this person to help me find, know, heal and forgive myself . I give to You my relationship with (NAME) and I thank You for taking us both and holding us in Your loving arms, that together we may remember all that is truthful, and learn to forget all that is false. I give to You my mistaken belief that I am separate from You, from (NAME) or from anyone and I give to you my desire to remember that I am One with You with (NAME) and with everyone. I thank You for Your courage and Your strength which bursts forth from within me, helping me to truly commit to love, to commit to union, to commit to peace and to commit to joy in this and in every relationship. For it is my will and Yours that I be free, that I be happy, and that I be at peace. Thank You........

Amen"

Adapted from a prayer found in a pamphlet by Miranda Holden (now Miranda Macpherson) in 1999.

About the Author

John Campbell

John is a Master Mariner and former ship's captain and spent over thirty years in the petrochemical industry until the stress of his life brought him to his knees in 1997 when his journey of awakening began.

He gave up all his business practices and began studying the human mind. He qualified as a Hypnotherapist and NLP Practitioner and undertook numerous trainings in his search for the meaning to life. After many years of studying various holistic and alternative healing modalities and undergoing intense healing of his own he came across *A Course in Miracles* (ACIM). He had a deep sense that this was something that he needed to study but found the book extremely challenging at first.

Two years later he read *The Disappearance of The Universe* by Gary Renard. This book explained in great detail what *A Course in Miracles* was truly trying to teach and convinced him to begin studying this metaphysical masterpiece in earnest.

John rented a room in a house and spent 18 months really studying ACIM and doing the daily lessons and practicing forgiveness in his daily life. Once he experienced the inner peace which the Course guarantees he was 'hooked.'

John is a former Director and Vice Chairman of Brighton & Hove Albion Football Club and he maintains his interest in the sport, generally, and in the club in particular. He has recently been introducing the principles of ACIM and the power of the mind to professional football coaches and players.

He is a world traveler, having been born in India and lived in South Africa, Kenya, Nigeria, Canada, Australia, Malaysia, Ireland and Spain.

John lives with his wife, Dr. Anne Campbell, author of the best-selling books under her previous married name of Moir, *Brain Sex, Why Men Don't Iron* and *A Mind To Crime*.

Dr. Anne Campbell is a former BAFTA award winner for her documentary making and is now working on a documentary with John about INNOCENT SEX.

info@miraclesrock.com
www.miraclesrock.com

Additional Websites

Sexual Re-Education:
www.innocentsex.org

O-BOOKS

SPIRITUALITY

O is a symbol of the world, of oneness and unity; this eye represents knowledge and insight. We publish titles on general spirituality and living a spiritual life. We aim to inform and help you on your own journey in this life.

If you have enjoyed this book, why not tell other readers by posting a review on your preferred book site?

Recent bestsellers from O-Books are:

Heart of Tantric Sex
Diana Richardson
Revealing Eastern secrets of deep love and intimacy to Western couples.
Paperback: 978-1-90381-637-0 ebook: 978-1-84694-637-0

Crystal Prescriptions
The A-Z guide to over 1,200 symptoms and their healing crystals
Judy Hall
The first in the popular series of eight books, this handy little guide is packed as tight as a pill-bottle with crystal remedies for ailments.
Paperback: 978-1-90504-740-6 ebook: 978-1-84694-629-5

Take Me To Truth
Undoing the Ego
Nouk Sanchez, Tomas Vieira
The best-selling step-by-step book on shedding the Ego, using the
teachings of *A Course In Miracles*.
Paperback: 978-1-84694-050-7 ebook: 978-1-84694-654-7

The 7 Myths about Love...Actually!
The Journey from your HEAD to the HEART of your SOUL
Mike George
Smashes all the myths about LOVE.
Paperback: 978-1-84694-288-4 ebook: 978-1-84694-682-0

The Holy Spirit's Interpretation of the New Testament
A Course in Understanding and Acceptance
Regina Dawn Akers
Following on from the strength of *A Course In Miracles*, NTI
teaches us how to experience the love and oneness of God.
Paperback: 978-1-84694-085-9 ebook: 978-1-78099-083-5

The Message of A Course In Miracles
A translation of the Text in plain language
Elizabeth A. Cronkhite
A translation of *A Course In Miracles* into plain, everyday
language for anyone seeking inner peace. The companion
volume, *Practicing A Course In Miracles*, offers practical lessons
and mentoring.
Paperback: 978-1-84694-319-5 ebook: 978-1-84694-642-4

Your Simple Path
Find Happiness in every step
Ian Tucker
A guide to helping us reconnect with what is really important in
our lives.
Paperback: 978-1-78279-349-6 ebook: 978-1-78279-348-9

365 Days of Wisdom
Daily Messages To Inspire You Through The Year
Dadi Janki
Daily messages which cool the mind, warm the heart and guide
you along your journey.
Paperback: 978-1-84694-863-3 ebook: 978-1-84694-864-0

Body of Wisdom
Women's Spiritual Power and How it Serves
Hilary Hart
Bringing together the dreams and experiences of women across
the world with today's most visionary spiritual teachers.
Paperback: 978-1-78099-696-7 ebook: 978-1-78099-695-0

Dying to Be Free
From Enforced Secrecy to Near Death to True Transformation
Hannah Robinson
After an unexpected accident and near-death experience, Hannah
Robinson found herself radically transforming her life, while a
remarkable new insight altered her relationship with her father, a
practising Catholic priest.
Paperback: 978-1-78535-254-6 ebook: 978-1-78535-255-3

The Ecology of the Soul
A Manual of Peace, Power and Personal Growth for Real People
in the Real World
Aidan Walker
Balance your own inner Ecology of the Soul to regain your
natural state of peace, power and wellbeing.
Paperback: 978-1-78279-850-7 ebook: 978-1-78279-849-1

Not I, Not other than I
The Life and Teachings of Russel Williams
Steve Taylor, Russel Williams
The miraculous life and inspiring teachings of one of the World's
greatest living Sages.
Paperback: 978-1-78279-729-6 ebook: 978-1-78279-728-9

On the Other Side of Love
A woman's unconventional journey towards wisdom
Muriel Maufroy
When life has lost all meaning, what do you do?
Paperback: 978-1-78535-281-2 ebook: 978-1-78535-282-9

Practicing A Course In Miracles
A translation of the Workbook in plain language, with
mentor's notes
Elizabeth A. Cronkhite
The practical second and third volumes of The Plain-Language
A Course In Miracles.
Paperback: 978-1-84694-403-1 ebook: 978-1-78099-072-9

Quantum Bliss

The Quantum Mechanics of Happiness, Abundance, and Health

George S. Mentz

Quantum Bliss is the breakthrough summary of success and spirituality secrets that customers have been waiting for.

Paperback: 978-1-78535-203-4 ebook: 978-1-78535-204-1

The Upside Down Mountain

Mags MacKean

A must-read for anyone weary of chasing success and happiness – one woman's inspirational journey swapping the uphill slog for the downhill slope.

Paperback: 978-1-78535-171-6 ebook: 978-1-78535-172-3

Your Personal Tuning Fork

The Endocrine System

Deborah Bates

Discover your body's health secret, the endocrine system, and 'twang' your way to sustainable health!

Paperback: 978-1-84694-503-8 ebook: 978-1-78099-697-4

Readers of ebooks can buy or view any of these bestsellers by clicking on the live link in the title. Most titles are published in paperback and as an ebook. Paperbacks are available in traditional bookshops. Both print and ebook formats are available online.

Find more titles and sign up to our readers' newsletter at http://www.johnhuntpublishing.com/mind-body-spirit

Follow us on Facebook at https://www.facebook.com/OBooks/ and Twitter at https://twitter.com/obooks